Is Your Job Search In Trouble?

by

I0463480

Randall C. Scasny

First Edition

Is Your Job Search In Trouble?

First Printing: 2016

ISBN: ISBN: 978-1-365-19798-7

Book Title: Is Your Job Search In Trouble?

HowToGetHiredQuickly.com

872 S. Milwaukee Ave. #261

Libertyville, IL 60048

This book is dedicated to my father, Frank C. Scasny.

Dawn points, and another day
Prepares for heat and silence. Out at sea the dawn wind
Wrinkles and slides. I am here
Or there, or elsewhere. In my beginning.
--TS Eliot

But O the ship, the immortal ship! O ship aboard the ship!
O ship of the body—ship of the soul—voyaging, voyaging, voyaging.
--Walt Whitman

Our boat is safely anchored by the shore,
And there will safely ride when we are gone;
The flowering shrubs that deck our humble door
Will prosper, though untended and alone.
--William Wordsworth

Table of Contents

Essential Terms

This book contains terms that are likely to be unfamiliar to some readers yet are essential to understanding the information and concepts discussed. I have listed the definitions of essential terms here.

Online Recruitment: any electronic intermediary between an individual job seeker and an employer. It can include: email; job boards; recruiting agency websites; staffing firm websites; newspaper classified websites; governmental career (workforce development) websites; corporate career sites; social media recruiting sites; professional association websites; message board lists; industry newsletters; and Internet blogs.

Job Board: the informal name applied to a website that contains databases of résumés and job ads. Job seekers search the job ad database for current openings, while employers or recruiters search the résumé database for job candidates to interview.

Social Recruiting Sites: the name applied to websites that use social media for career transitions. Like job boards, they contain candidate profiles and résumés, as well as job ads. Recruiters primarily use social recruiting sites to search for candidates by keywords; however, the connections that candidates develop can also be a sourcing pool for recruiters. In addition, recruiters also use social recruiting sites to learn more about a candidate, basically, as an informal background check. The important difference between a job board and a social recruiting site is that members of social recruiting sites can connect with other members. This networking may generate referrals and job leads.

Recruiter: a sales person or representative, who is usually compensated by employers, and acts as a "gate keeper" in the hiring process. There are different types of recruiters. Executive recruiters or "headhunters" are the most well known. They work with high-wage job seekers and obtain *large* commissions when they place an executive with an employer. Technical recruiters work with technical professionals and perform a role similar to that of an executive recruiter. Some recruiters work for staffing agencies; these people are on salary and generally do not earn large commissions. Instead, they work on behalf of their client, the employer, to find appropriate job candidates. Offshore recruiters are the newest type of recruiter. They work for companies based outside of the U.S. who are seeking U.S. workers to fill their U.S. positions primarily due to the limitations the U.S. government places on guest worker visas, such as H1-bs.

Sourcing: all actions taken by both recruiters and hiring managers to find people for open positions. Sourcing is synonymous with "selecting" or "finding." In the past, recruiters and hiring managers used mainly contacts they had developed through networked "human relationships" to source candidates. Nowadays, recruiters usually source candidates by using keyword searches of résumé databases from job boards and connections from social recruiting sites.

Résumé Database: a database "warehouse" of career information of both active and passive job candidates. They contain as few as a couple of thousand résumés to as many as 300 Million or more.

Online Résumé: a résumé written specifically for a résumé database. It emphasizes information and keywords over visual format. These résumés are much longer than the traditional one-page résumé. In theory, they are limitless since the length of a résumé does not really matter for a database; however, most online résumés are two to four pages long.

Résumé Visibility: when a résumé obtains high ranking in résumé database searches. High ranking equals high visibility, which usually translates into frequent callbacks by recruiters who view the résumé in an online recruitment database.

Online Recruitment Tools

It can be confusing for job seekers new to online recruitment to understand what online tools, websites, and social recruiting sites to use since there are different types of online recruitment tools and websites. To clarify matters, let me begin with some definitions of the different types of sites, which will give you a context to understand all online recruitment sites. Online recruitment tools and websites are divided into the following categories:

- General-Purpose Job Boards
- Market Niche Job Boards
- Social Recruiting Sites
- Job Ad Aggregator Sites
- Online Contract Bidding Networks
- Employer-Hosted Career Sites

General-purpose job boards are multi-industry, job listing websites that contain two types of databases: a résumé database and a job ad database. Employers search the résumé database for job candidates while job seekers search the job ad database to find job openings. Monster.com is a typical example of a job board in this category.

Market niche job boards are identical to general-purpose boards with one important difference: they focus on only one type of industry or occupation. *Hcareers.com*, which covers the hospitality industry, and *Dice.com*, which covers the information technology industry, are typical examples.

Social recruiting sites are a hybrid of social media and general-purpose job boards. But instead of a résumé database, these sites have a member-profile database that contains not only a résumé but also a lot of personal information about the members. Recruiters are transitioning from relying on job boards to using social recruiting sites because these sites provide more information about job seekers. Finally, social recruiting sites enable relationship-building between members and recruiters, which to a degree can impact a job seeker's ability to get hired quickly. LinkedIn.com is a typical example.

Job ad aggregator sites look like general-purpose job boards but are really "job ad" search engines that index job ads from job boards, company career sites, staffing agencies, etc. and place them onto one website for convenience. When a job seeker clicks on a job, she is sent to the source of the ad. Job ad aggregators can speed up the process of finding job openings, but they can also be very competitive. The larger ones get a lot of traffic and can generate lots of job applicants. Indeed.com is a typical example.

Online contract bidding networks are a relatively new concept for obtaining employment. One could call these sites "task-based" job boards. Their structure is similar to a job board. The big difference is the type of jobs posted. Most of the jobs are either single-task jobs, or jobs that will last for a few days to a few weeks. The employer may be a large company, small business or an individual who needs a specific task done such as, write a business plan, update a page on a website, write a piece of software code, proofread a document, or design a website logo. On these networks, job seekers can get employed in a few hours from the time of application – a definite advantage! However, the pay structure is very different than other types of employment. These networks use bidding to determine compensation; the bidding process is intended to mimic contract bidding in the B2B marketplace. This is how bidding works: The job seeker applies for a job and raises or lowers her "bid salary" based upon the competition or the complexity of the job. The website offers credibility ratings: as the job seeker gains credibility, over a period of time, she can command a higher wage. It should be noted that the job seeker controls the wage of compensation, not the employer. This type of employment is turning into big business. It will be the employment mode of the future, as more and more work will be accomplished via telecommuting. Upwork.com is a typical example.

Employer-hosted career sites are job boards hosted on an employer's website. An example of a career site is Allstate.com, the insurance company. To find these career sites, go to the employer's website. This can be done by using your favorite Web search engine (e.g., Bing, Google, etc.) and perform a search using the following keywords to search: *[Company name] + Careers.*

Is Your Job Search In Trouble?

Have you been looking for a job for several months and don't feel you're any closer to a job offer than when you began months ago?

Well, you are not alone. Nearly all job seekers today experience under-performing job searches and don't always understand why.

In the past, job search campaigns were defined in days or weeks. But recent employment statistics say that people are now remaining unemployed for many months, with a large portion of job seekers staying unemployed for a year or more.

Why are qualified job candidates today having problems getting hired? The experts debate the causes of long-term job searches. Economists claim there are too many job seekers for too few jobs. Newspapers claim it is the slow economy and look to Congress for solutions. Educators blame the U.S. educational system, alleging it is not preparing new graduates with the skills needed for high-demand jobs. Some politicians even blame the unemployed themselves!

We can all argue about the causes of long-term unemployment, but few of us would deny the path for getting hired is harder and longer than it once was.

What the experts, the press, educators, and politicians fail to consider is the effect that technology has on getting hired.

Over the past decade, the art of job seeking has turned into a "data science," featuring advanced technologies that employers use to hunt down, select, pre-screen, interview and extensively "profile" job applicants. These technologies purposely create hyper-competition, making it that much harder for millions of people to get hired in a reasonable length of time.

Job boards, social media sites and Internet career portals are implementing advanced "online recruitment" technologies so rapidly that human intervention is being removed from the hiring process. Advanced online recruitment technologies now control (1) how job candidates are defined as "qualified," (2) how résumés are selected for recruiter callbacks and in-person interviews and (3) how hiring decisions are made and job offers tendered.

This book proposes solutions to the problems associated with long-term job search campaigns. If you aren't getting phone calls from recruiters or interviews at an employer's office in the first month of your job search, then this book is written for you.

This book will teach you not only how to identify if your job search is in trouble, it will also teach you how to solve your problems quickly so you save time and prevent months of fruitless effort in looking for a job.

1. How Well Is Your Job Search Performing?

How do you turnaround a slow-motion job search campaign and make it into a thriving one with frequent callbacks, regular interviews, and quick job offers? The first step is to understand how well your job search is performing right now. To do so, ask yourself these questions:

- How long have you been looking for a job?
- How many callbacks have you received for jobs specific to your occupation?
- How many in-person interviews have you had?

If your job search is performing well, you should be getting calls by recruiters who need someone with your skills and background within the first week or two of the launch of your job search campaign. You should also be getting an in-person interview every other week over a 3-month period.

If you are not getting enough callbacks or in-person interviews, your job search will be stretched out by months. It is very important to get responses from your résumé postings, job applications, and social recruiting profiles because a job search campaign is a numbers game. To get a job offer, you need to get in-person interviews; to get in-person interviews, you need to be called back. Few callbacks generate few interviews, which generate few if any job offers.

Online Requirement Requires New Job Search Tactics

Prior to the widespread adoption of online recruitment, the most common solutions to employment problems were (1) get more education, (2) move to a new location that has better prospects for employment, or (3) do more networking to build up professional connections with people who can refer you to a prospective employer. For the most part, these solutions may still improve your prospects of getting hired; unfortunately, their impact is not always immediate.

While I would never discourage a job seeker from pursuing more education and training, earning college degree alone does not always translate into a quick job offer. Hiring decisions today are based upon more than educational credentials. The supply and demand of a local marketplace and the specific needs of employers have much more influence on hiring decisions than credentials alone.

A more effective approach is to focus on the "here and now" to determine exactly why you can't find a job now with your current education, skills, and present location.

The Best Way to Solve a Job Search Problem

How do most people define a "job search" problem? It's been my experience that most people define them in terms of skill gaps, a lack of a college degree, wrong location, or a lack of inside connections. While these things influence unemployment, they are not a comprehensive list, nor are they necessarily the primary cause of a job search problem for a specific individual at a specific time and in a specific location. In addition, they are generic in nature and do not tell you what your problem is. So, I suggest a different approach.

Instead of viewing the solution to your job search problem in terms of skills, education, location, I have found that it is better to look at what you have done – your job seeking behavior – to determine why you have had a very slow and unsuccessful job search campaign. Start by reviewing the observable actions you have taken over the course of your job search and the results they have obtained for you. If you do, you will find that there are *only* three universal job-seeking problems. They are:

The "No Calls" Problem

Job seekers describe this problem in the following way: "I am not getting any phone calls for interviews after I apply to jobs or post my résumé online. It feels like I have a dead job hunt."

The "No Interviews" Problem

Job seekers describe this problem in the following way: "I am getting telephone calls from my résumé postings and job applications but I am not being invited to in-person interviews at the employer's office."

The "No Job Offer" Problem

Job seekers describe this problem in the following way: "I am invited to in-person interviews but never get a job offer."

Setting Achievable Goals Is Key To Your Success

By breaking down a job search campaign into these three problems, job seekers have (1) a metric to gauge their progress and (2) a structure to set achievable and incremental goals.

If you understand each of these behavioral-driven, job-search problems and how to correct them, you can learn how to take specific actions to propel your job search campaign forward quickly.

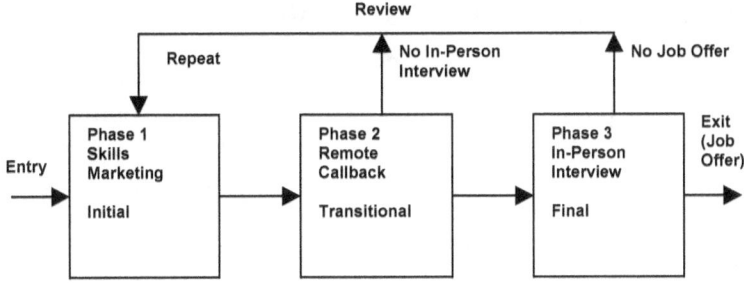

The above diagram is a visual representation of the three universal job-seeking problems. Here's how it works:

- When a job seeker begins a job search, she enters Phase 1, the skills marketing phase, where she uses her résumé to connect with employers for job interviews.

- Upon receiving callbacks, she takes remote pre-screening calls in Phase 2 to obtain in-person interviews.

- Upon receiving in-person interviews, she either receives a job offer and exits the job search, or makes adjustments to repeat the process until she receives a job offer.

2. How to Solve a "No Calls" Problem

The "No Calls" problem is the most common problem confronting job seekers today. What is a "No Calls" problem? It is when job seekers spend nearly all their time in pre-interview, skills-marketing activities – applying for jobs, posting résumés online, rewriting résumés, etc. – but get few if any callbacks for job opportunities *specific* to their skills and experience.

Most people who experience a "No Calls" problem blame their résumé so they either rewrite it or get someone to do it for them. While a poorly written résumé can cause a "No Calls" problem, it is by no means the only cause of it.

The best way to solve a "No Calls" problem is to do the following:

- Determine if your résumé has a low visibility problem.

- Verify that your résumé database postings, job application submittals or online interviews (supplemental questionnaires) are not somehow eliminating you as a candidate.

- Research your local job market to ensure there is adequate job demand for your occupational specialty.

Determine if your résumé has a low visibility problem

The first step in solving a "No Calls" problem is to determine if employers are viewing your résumé. If not, you have a résumé with low visibility; it is ranked too low to be viewed in a database search.

An easy résumé-visibility test is to upload your résumé to a résumé database on a general-purpose job board that tracks résumé searches, saves, or views such as CareerBuilder.com or Monster.com. Log into your account a few days after you uploaded it and check the results. If your résumé has few searches or views, it usually means the résumé has low visibility and needs to be rewritten.

Generally speaking, résumés with low visibility are not structured the same way the résumé database is structured, making its information difficult to be found in database searches. Always structure your résumé with the same and corresponding fields of a database. If a résumé database has a job-title field, then your résumé must have a job-title section in it. If the résumé database has a certifications field, your résumé must have a certifications section in it. And so on.

Low visibility résumés also have another problem: they do not have enough detail. A lack of detail creates a lack of keywords. Without enough keywords, your résumé will receive a lower ranking than others. So, rewrite your résumé. After rewriting it, delete the current one, re-post your new résumé, and test it again. Keep doing this until you see the searches and views increase.

Verify that your résumé database postings or job application submittals are not eliminating you as a candidate.

Many times it is not your résumé *per se* that is causing a "No Calls" problem, but the way your résumé is posted or entered into the database.

Uploading a résumé to a database is not difficult, but often the software does not populate the database fields correctly. It pays to go back and check each field to ensure that your information was entered properly.

Pay special attention to job titles and company names since they are rich keywords. Keywords are the key to getting on the radar screen of recruiters. These are words that recruiters will likely use as search terms when narrowing a field of job candidates for a job she is trying to fill.

Work status is another important piece of information; ensure you have selected a status that says you are legally eligible to work.

Avoid listing your salary history in an online résumé profile. If you have indicated a salary outside of the employer's range, you will not be called.

Select as many employment types and work shifts as possible. You can always change your preferences after a recruiter contacts you.

The next step is to maximize your job skills, which are your primary keywords. "Harvest" as many keywords as you can from job ads and insert them into your résumé. They should, of course, be appropriate to your occupation and skills.

Be creative in how you define your skills. Many times people limit their skills to software. It is much better to go through a job ad and highlight every unique phrase. If a phrase applies to you, consider listing it as a skill in your résumé or social recruiting profile.

You shouldn't bother listing your geographical preferences, other than your local zip code. Unless you have rare skills, you will not be contacted for non-local jobs.

Do not include a cover letter for résumé database postings – no one reads them. However, a cover letter should be included in a job application. Only include a photo if it is a business-wear photo. (No Hawaiian shirts, please!)

Research your local job market

A local job market can cause a "No Calls" problem if the need for your occupational specialty is low. Search for jobs using your job title keywords.

If you see few postings, you should suspect that the local job demand is low. Next, take a look at the job statistics at the U.S. Department of Labor, Bureau of Labor Statistics website (www.bls.gov). Specifically, look at the Economies at a Glance section for the metro area nearest to you. Study the 12-month changes. If you see a decrease or a leveling-off in jobs, low job demand is a likely cause and at least part of your problem.

The best way to solve a low job demand problem is to either (a) wait for demand in your local market to increase, or (b) choose a new job or occupation that has a higher level of demand.

Eliminate any additional factors

If you have eliminated your résumé, how you post your résumé to databases, and local job demand factors as the causes of your "No Calls" problem, then you must look at the additional factors (other than your résumé) that may be causing this problem. These external causes are discussed in the next chapter.

3. The Additional Causes of "No Calls" Problems

Nearly 100 percent of job seekers who experience a "No Calls" problem attribute it to an ineffective résumé. While it is true that an ineffective résumé can cause a "No Calls" problem, it isn't the only cause. This chapter describes the 14 additional causes of the "No Calls" problem other than an ineffective résumé.

1) Applying to jobs for which you are not fully qualified

Many job seekers do not read job ads closely, so they do not fully understand the employer's job requirements. The description of the job requirements in a job ad is where recruiters find the keywords for their résumé-database searches. So, if you apply to jobs where you do not have at least 80 percent of the employer's job requirements, no matter how good a résumé you think you have, you are likely to obtain low ranking (poor résumé visibility) and few if any callbacks. Do not apply to jobs for which you are largely unqualified. Avoid applying to large numbers of jobs for which you are only partially qualified in the hope that employers will call you (and train you). It's unlikely they will. They are looking for job candidates who meet all or almost all of their requirements.

2) Incomplete job candidate profile

Online recruitment portals, such as job boards and social recruiting sites, contain a lot of information. They have contact information, career objectives, salary information, location preferences, job types, skills, work experience and much more. This information is collected for a reason. It allows the recruiter to review your profile as an "online interview" in order to pre-screen you for a job she is trying to fill *without* actually calling you. In other words, as recruiters search résumé databases, their searches function as *virtual* interviews. If you are not being contacted, the cause could be the lack of information you provided in your online profile. The best way to solve this problem is to complete your profile.

3) Job candidacy eliminated by a pre-employment questionnaire

Employers now use online assessments as a pre-screening mechanism. They can ask job candidates many more questions than could be asked in either phone or in-person interviews. Online assessments are usually embedded within job applications. They include questions about your credentials and your specific level of experience. Based upon your answers to the questions, you will be eliminated or passed on to the next screening level. The best way to respond to pre-employment questions is to prepare your answers in advance of entering them. A typical pre-employment questionnaire may consist of the following questions:

- What are the greatest strengths you bring to your job?

- What traits or characteristics in co-workers do you most dislike?

- What was the best job you've ever had? Why did you like it so much?

- What was the least favorite job you've ever had? Why did you dislike it?

- List all the office software you know.

- What is the most difficult part of managing the work of others?

- What is the most difficult personnel decision you have ever had to make?

- How do you want to be managed?

- What won't you do?

- What strategies have you used to ensure customer satisfaction?

- What is the most innovative technique you have ever used to solve a problem?

- Describe what each of the following means to you: responsibility, empowerment, accountability, and leadership.

4) Misspelled words or incorrect grammar

One of the challenges employers face in an oversupplied talent market is pruning their long list of job candidates. One simple way to eliminate candidates is to filter out those who demonstrate a lack of basic writing skills. Grammatical errors and misspelled words can eliminate your job candidacy immediately. Use both the spell checker of your word processor and have someone else read your résumé to see if there are any spelling or grammatical problems. Spell checkers have limitations so do not rely on them alone to catch errors. Subscribe to grammar-checking applications such as *Grammarly* to help you correct errors.

5) Applying after the closing date

Online recruitment allows recruiters to distribute job ads widely. In theory, this gives job seekers many opportunities to apply for jobs. On the face of it, online recruitment seems to have created many new opportunities for job applicants. However, this freedom sometimes obscures the limitations and restrictions set by employers. One of these restrictions is the closing date, which is the final date when a job application will be accepted. If you send your job application after the closing date, your job candidacy will be disqualified. Again, carefully read the job ad. If there is a closing date, it will say so.

6) Not identifying your work status or proof of eligibility to work

Almost all job applications today ask questions regarding a candidate's work status, eligibility to work, or need of a work visa sponsorship. Online recruitment, along with the e-verify program (the Federal program that employers use to verify that workers are eligible to work), quickly filters out applicants who are ineligible to work. Employment within the U.S. Federal government has additional eligibility requirements: you may be a U.S. citizen and eligible to work in the U.S., but you may not be eligible to apply for certain jobs in the Federal Government because they require Federal "competitive status." For more information, see the eligibility requirements at *USAjobs.gov.*

7) Local job candidates are preferred over non-local candidates

All online job applications give you the option of indicating if you want to relocate and what your relocation preferences are. You may think that applying to an out-of-area job is a good way to move. Well, consider this: just because you can apply to out-of-area jobs does not mean you will be considered a serious candidate.

Prior to online recruitment, high-demand job candidates would be flown anywhere in the United States for a job interview. Why? Employers did not have a lot of job candidates from which to choose – there were no globally accessible résumé databases before online recruitment began in 1997. With a relatively small talent pool, employers were willing to compete for job candidates. This happens infrequently now. Millions of job candidates have posted their career information online, and many geographical areas have large pools of talent. As a result, recruiters often conduct zip code searches for potential job candidates. If your profile does not have a local zip code for the job a recruiter is trying to fill, you will likely be eliminated from consideration.

To solve this challenge, focus your job search campaign on your local area. If the local job market is weak, then expand your job search campaign to out-of-area jobs.

If you must move, then you have to ask yourself how would you present yourself as a local job candidate. One way would be to ask a friend or family member who lives in that area if you could use their address. Since it normally takes a few weeks to get a callback and a few more weeks to set up an in-person interview, you have plenty of time to make travel arrangements when an interview offer does arise. During an interview, if the subject of your home-of-record is brought up, you can say you are currently in the process of moving.

8) Applying to a "contract pending" job or a "fake" job ad

Some job postings are annotated with the phrase "Pending Contract Approval." This is a dead giveaway for a "résumé-collecting" job ad. What this means is that the employer is bidding on a contract (usually a Federal contract or project-oriented work at an ad agency) and when it wins the contract, it needs to hire people quickly to meet the contract's requirements. But unless and until the contract is awarded, employers won't be hiring. You may need to wait months to get a phone call for a pending-contract-approval job.

A variation of the "contract pending" job ad is the "fake" job ad, which is a job ad that is posted on a website, but is never taken down. It will appear to be a permanent fixture on the employer's website. If a job ad has been posted for over 6 months, it's more than likely a fake ad.

9) Career change to a different industry or occupation

People often change careers over the course of their work lives. Prior to the widespread use of online recruitment, this was not a problem because there were small talent pools and employers would consider anyone who appeared to be reasonable and could be trained quickly.

Times have changed: unless it is really necessary, employers don't want to train people today. A career change to a different job or industry creates a problem for job seekers if they require retraining by an employer. An employer would rather search massive résumé databases for the perfect yet nonexistent job candidate than one who needs even a little training.

The best way to deal with this problem is to make a lateral move to a new company and look for new opportunities there to move up and into a different position. For example, let's say you are a logistics analyst who wants to become a supply chain manager. The best way to make this career change is to look outside your current employer for jobs similar to a logistics analyst (lateral move) in companies where it appears you can see career growth. But once you are employed in the new company, seek to transition to another occupation or career level as an internal candidate (upward move). This approach may take some time, but it generally is more effective than spending many months of applying to jobs as an external candidate in a career change.

10) Not enough time to process the application

It takes most employers up to one month after getting your résumé or closing a job to call candidates for a job interview. (In some instances employers will not call for six months!) Why so long? There are a number of reasons. The employer may have run a job ad and then decided it did not want to hire at that time so it held onto the job applications until it was ready. Furthermore, an employer may post a job to its own career site as well as up to five other job boards and social recruiting sites. It takes about two weeks to collect résumés and another week for review. During the next week, they will make calls to the best candidates. The first interviews occur in the fourth week. If you are expecting a response in a few days to a week, you have not given the employer enough time to process your application.

11) Not passing the background checks

With a steady supply of job candidates, employers spend more time pre-screening candidates than they did ten years ago. Moreover, employers are now using FBI databases to conduct criminal background checks. The problem with FBI databases is that they contain arrest records, but not the disposition (convictions) of those arrests, making the information in them inconclusive. The FBI does not generate the information itself – it gets the information from each state. FBI databases are known to have inaccurate information yet employers still use them.

Credit, work reference, and social media checks are being increasingly conducted by employers prior to contacting job candidates. If you have a credit problem or low credit score, you may filtered out. (This can happen simply because you own a home and have a large debt load.)

Criminal background checks can be a job killer. Even a DUI conviction in some states can kill your job candidacy. In addition, employers are rewriting employment applications in such a manner to include dismissed charges or arrests/convictions beyond the statute of limitations dictated by state law. These can all add up to a "No Calls" problem.

Drug tests given early in the hiring process can also turn into a "No Calls" problem. This problem is on the rise due to the increased accuracy of drug tests and the greater prevalence of job candidates who have used now legal recreational drugs. While you may live in a state where recreational drug use is allowed, an employer may have set its own "no tolerance" policy that can eliminate your candidacy.

There is no easy way to get around background check problems in the published, competitive job market. If you suspect that not passing the background checks is the cause of your "No Calls" problem, you will either need to do some networking to obtain employment in the unpublished or hidden job market, or work with organizations that place people who have background problems such as felony convictions. Being terminated or "fired" is another problem. There will be employers who filter you out for being fired, sacked or terminated.

Social media site information can eliminate your job candidacy and give you a "No Calls" problem. Despite the buzz about how social recruiting is changing the way people get hired, the amount of hiring through these sites is currently small relative the super-large talent pool that is made available via social recruiting sites. But even when employers are not using social recruiting sites to source candidates, they are using them as soft background checks to vet potential hires. In other words, social recruiting "checks" are an influencer in hiring decisions.

Unflattering information on a social recruiting site, including the ads and the content that appears on your page, can create a negative perception and kill your job candidacy. The best way to overcome this problem is to (a) limit the personal information you place on your social media profile, (b) create a private social media site for job searching purposes that has only career information posted, (c) "unfriend" people who generate weird content on your profile, or (d) increase the security of your profile so that only your connections or friends can see your profile. This will prevent recruiters from seeing your profile. (I have tested this last approach. What happens is that if a recruiter can't see or find your profile, she will give you a call, which is what you want her to do!)

12) Above the employer's salary range

One of the unfortunate consequences of online recruitment is basic economics: when supply is much higher than demand, prices slump. With a large supply of talent available through résumé databases, employers have found they can pay less for workers. Only occupations that require truly rare skills will pay top dollar.

In addition, employers are hiring temporary workers more than ever before, so the average salary workers earn today tends to be lower than it used to be. In the end, if an employer requires you to submit a salary history AND you are above the employer's salary range, you are likely to experience a "No Calls" problem unless you have rare, high-demand skills.

The best way to overcome this problem is to avoid mentioning your salary if possible. When required, choose a range that spans at least part of the employer's salary range. You should research salaries being paid in your area for your occupation before listing a salary on an application.

Keep in mind that government statistics on salaries will generally be lower than what you read on popular websites such as *Salary.com* or *Glassdoor.com*. Government statistics utilize large samples and are averaged while "salary" hearsay on career-oriented websites does not always represent the entire U.S working population so its information is inaccurate. What you want to do is get into the ballpark salary range and get an interview. Once you are offered a job, you can begin negotiating for your compensation.

13) A lack of "job title" experience

Recruiters often search for candidates by using a location (zip code) and the job title for the position they are trying to fill. Most of the time, they are only interested in calling job candidates who have "recent" and "proven" job title experience. Now it is quite possible that you have the skills for a particular job yet you have never actually held the job. This is often the case with seasoned military veterans, some new graduates, or mid-to-late career changers. A lack of job title experience surfaces as a problem when we consider how résumé search engines rank résumés in database searches. Those candidates who have actual job title experience will be ranked higher than those who have not held that job title previously. So, you could very well have the skills to perform the duties of the job (and you could in fact be more qualified than those candidates who have previously held the job), yet your résumé will be ranked lower than other candidates who have the desired job title experience. If your résumé is ranked lower than others, there is a likelihood you will be so far down in the search findings that you will not be called.

14) Employers who are "lemons" will never call you

Most job seekers respect employers and believe them to be honest and have sound core values. This first impression is natural, but it is also a bit naïve. Like any relationship – work, romance, hobbies, etc. – one starts the relationship with high hopes of fair play. As the relationship develops, however, things may change. Actions speak louder than words. Some employers and recruiters are real "lemons." They don't get back to you. They cancel appointments or misrepresent the job in the ad. They may be dishonest or bullies. The list of immature and insensitive behavior is almost endless. Luckily, the group of lemon employers is small. The best thing to do is recognize one when you see one and move on.

4. The "No Calls" Problem: Is Social Media The Answer?

In a very short period of time, social media has become an important part of our lives. We use it to keep in touch or get in touch with old school friends, distant relatives or even military buddies. We use it to post family photos. We even use social media in the political process.

Since the most popular social media sites (e.g., Facebook, Linkedin, etc.) allow you to post your résumé in your member profile, it's natural for someone searching for a job to use social media as part of his or her job search.

Is the use of social media an effective tool in getting the long-term unemployed hired again? Well, try this test: ask ten people you know who are looking for a job whether they know someone who has gotten hired as a *direct* result of a social recruiting site. You'll find that the common response is "No. I don't really know anyone who has."

This response runs counter to the frequent news reports that claim employers are hiring more through social media. The only explanation for this contradiction is that *some* people but *not* most of the millions of job seekers in the U.S. are getting hired as a direct result of social media. Too few jobs are being created and too much talent is available for that to happen. Most studies have placed the hiring success rate of social media sites at about 5 percent.

Granted, some people do get hired through social media. Some of this hiring is the result of the transition from job-board-application hiring to social-recruiting-relationship hiring. In the near future you should expect there to be more social media hiring as the hiring via traditional job boards wanes. It will probably max out at 10-15%, however. This is the level of hiring on most job boards today. (Note: People who are new to online recruitment are often surprised at the low level of hiring of the online job portals. This is primarily due to the fact that most of the information that's written about online recruitment is provided by the public relations *machines* of the job sites themselves! They have a business interest in making their sites appear more successful than they really are. Of course, this is pure hype.)

The other reason some job seekers get hired through social media is that they are compelling job candidates. They usually earn very high incomes. Low-to-moderate income earners have much more job competition, so they have a harder time getting calls for interviews.

Always remember job seeking in any form is a numbers game: the higher the competition, the lower the hiring success rate.

Another less talked about reason why most people are unsuccessful in gaining employment through social media is that social recruiting is unregulated with no oversight. There is no means to track whether a recruiter that does database searches is following EEO guidelines or discriminating against a candidate because he or she is a certain race or gender. There is also no way to know whether a physically attractive job candidate is being chosen over a not so attractive candidate. There is even no way of knowing whether an Ivy League school graduate is being chosen over a Nebraska state college graduate. This circumstance will continue until professional standards are implemented in the online recruitment industry. Unfortunately, the U.S. Congress doesn't appear to want to get involved in this endeavor.

So, how can you use social media to your advantage in your pursuit of a new job?

It is unlikely that early-to-mid career workers have hundreds of connections within the social media world; they have not been in the working world long enough. But don't fret: online connections aren't as powerful as they are reported to be. Knowing a current employee who can refer you to a job is still a much more effective way to getting hired quickly than anything online recruitment can provide.

At the early-to-mid career level, it is best for a job seeker to treat his or her social media profile as if it were a job board profile. Post a detailed résumé. Post the maximum number of skills allowed – skill keywords are how recruiters will find you and contact you for interviews.

Use the optional sections for expanding and deepening your social media profile: projects, awards, courses, test scores, volunteer work, etc. Post a friendly yet professional photo – a headshot in business attire. Update your site daily with a targeted news story link in the industry or business line for which you are seeking employment. This will drive traffic to your profile. More eyeballs viewing your profile will increase the probability of getting a recruiter inquiry.

Since social media profiles are used as an informal pre-interview background check by recruiters, ensure that your social media résumé corresponds to the résumé you have posted on a job board or submitted with a job application. So, remove any questionable information.

5. How Résumés Are Ranked in Database Searches

Online recruitment has elevated the importance of résumé databases to new heights. They have become the primary means by which recruiters find job candidates. The simple fact is that databases of the most popular online job portals host hundreds of millions of résumés. This over-abundance of instant-access talent pools creates numerous opportunities for recruiters to find talent to call (or instantly reject if they don't match an employer's requirements).

Résumé databases create a level of competition so high that even well qualified job seekers can be eliminated. A job seeker can "fight" this high competition by gaining a better understanding of how databases rank résumés, which is the focus of this chapter.

Since a typical database search can return hundreds or even thousands of résumés in a single search, most recruiters will only look at the top findings – résumés that are ranked on the first or second page of the search findings. From a job seeker's perspective, top ranking is critical to avoid having a chronic "No Calls" problem.

Recruiters use the following parameters to find candidates in résumé databases:

- Job Title
- Location
- Industry
- Skill
- Company Name
- School Name

To understand how résumés are ranked in database searches, you need to understand the rule of the search function that's used to rank the search findings. Simply stated, the rule is:

The most ideal job candidate is a local candidate whose recent job-title experience corresponds to the job-title keywords and location used by a recruiter in a database search, and supported by less recent job-title experience that's documented within a résumé.

This rule means that the more recent job-title experience a job seeker has, the higher he or she will be placed in the search rankings. Job-title experience that occurred a few years ago or in the distant past will force a résumé lower than others in the search rankings with more recent job-title experience.

This rule creates many different search-ranking results and can seriously impact how a particular job seeker can rely on résumé databases to generate frequent calls for job interviews. Let us examine the effects of this rule on the most common types of database searches.

There are four different kinds of database searches. They are:

- **Primary**: job title + location
- **Industry Sensitive**: job title + location + industry
- **Skills Sensitive**: job title + location + skills
- **Relationship Sensitive**: job title + company + location (or job title + school name + location)

Primary Searches

The primary search is the most common and fundamental search conducted by a recruiter. The location means the recruiter is seeking a local job candidate. Therefore, non-local job candidates will be blind to a recruiter searching a résumé database because a zip code is used as the location identifier.

A recruiter will always use the job title of the position she is attempting to fill because she is trying to reduce the risk of working with candidates who are either partially or not qualified. So, even if you have the skills for a job, if you have not held the *actual* job title of the job being filled, your résumé will be ranked lower than someone who has in the past or is currently in that role.

This means that career changers, new graduates, military veterans, or anyone applying to a job that he or she has not *actually* held will be pushed down the rankings. This comes as a surprise to older career changers. In the past, (prior to the introduction of online recruitment) employers were more inclined to hire someone with good yet not exact job experience if the career changer demonstrated talent, abilities and relevant skills. This is not the case today.

If you have not held a job title recently, you will be ranked higher than candidates who have not had held it at all, but you will be ranked lower than a candidate who is currently holding that job title or who has held it more recently than yourself. This essentially says that recruiters only care about a candidate's most recent experience. Old experience is less important because it is perceived as outdated, rusty or stagnant.

Industry Sensitive Searches

Industry sensitive searches are similar to primary searches except that an additional condition is placed in the database search: job candidates who have specific industry experience in addition to job title experience will be pushed up the rankings. Industry experience is one of the new trends in employer selection requirements. Industry experience means you have worked in a particular environment that is important to an employer.

Skills Sensitive Searches

Skills sensitive searches are similar to primary searches except an additional condition is placed in the database search: job candidates who have a specific skill are ranked higher than similar candidates who do not. This type of search is not necessarily industry sensitive. For example, building or coding a website is generally not industry sensitive; however, a marketing analyst or content writer would be industry sensitive because these positions would require the employee to know something about the industry for which he or she is writing collaterals or building marketing campaigns. Skills sensitive positions are common in contract work.

Relationship Sensitive Searches

While not common, relationship sensitive searches exist because the recruiter wants to find candidates who have previously worked for a particular company or have graduated from a particular school. Job candidates with these requirements are preferred because the employer is looking for an "insider," not an external candidate who would need to learn their system or adapt to their work culture.

Who Are Recruiters Seeking in Database Searches?

In the end, the rule of database searches implies that recruiters primarily look for seasoned professionals for lateral career moves. They represent the least amount of risk and offer the highest possible returns for a recruiter (i.e. time saved and large commissions earned) who is seeking to place a job candidate with one of his or her clients.

6. How to Solve a "No Interviews" Problem

Once you solve your "No Calls" problem, you should begin receiving inquiries from recruiters and hiring managers on a regular basis. Generally speaking, if you receive an occupationally specific callback about once every ten days or so, the first phase of your job search campaign is healthy.

The purpose of the callback is to pre-screen you for a job opening based upon your résumé or job application. In the past, telephone pre-screening almost always resulted in an invitation for an in-person interview. That's not always the case today.

The pre-screening process has changed immensely and the pre-screening call now has much greater importance than it once did. Recruiting and human resource professionals have teamed with information technology experts to develop new ways of finding job candidates. This collaboration results in job candidates that not only match the employer's requirements, but also predicts the success of candidates in the position they are trying to fill.

The traditional factors of determining hiring success such as college reputation, degree, and grade point averages are fading away. They are slowly being replaced by videos, problem-solving competitions, and pre-employment questionnaires that raise the competitive bar considerably.

In addition, information technology has taken the pre-screening call to a level never before seen. Multiple calls utilizing various media are common. Pre-screening calls can include any or all of the following:

- Phone interviews
- Skype interviews
- Audio recordings
- Video recordings
- Online assessment tests
- Online chats

The pre-screening call has also expanded to a variety of interview methods that include:

- Situational interviews
- Technical interviews
- Reasoning assessments

- Psychological assessments
- Emotional and social assessments
- Meet-and-greet interviews

Technology enables employers to gather a great deal of detailed information about a job candidate without bringing the candidate to the employer's office. Only those candidates who pass this extensive pre-screening will be brought to the office for an in-person interview. This has increased the difficulty of moving out of the transitional phase into the final phase of a job search campaign.

If you are obtaining pre-screening calls, yet are not regularly being invited to in-person interviews, you have a "No In-Person Interviews" problem. This generally means something went wrong during the pre-screening call. Remember, if you received a callback, then your résumé is doing its job. So, don't go back and rewrite your résumé simply because you did not get offered an in-person interview after a phone screen.

To correct a "No In-Person Interviews" problem, let's start by discussing phone calls, which are still the most common type of pre-screening test, and follow up with tips that deal with other types of pre-screening mechanisms.

Pre-Screening Phone Calls

The purpose of a pre-screening call is to further narrow down the talent pool a recruiter has sourced from résumé postings, job applications, and referrals. Candidates who are not screened out during the pre-screening call will be invited to an in-person interview.

What happens to cause you to not receive in-person interview invitations? A lack of phone communication skills is a possibility, but not a leading reason. Many job seekers mistakenly attribute the "No In-Person Interviews" problem to a lack of phone communication skills, leading job seekers to take interview preparation "lessons" or participate in mock interviews.

To solve the "No In-Person Interviews" problem, you need to understand with whom you are speaking, and what is their goal. Many employers do not themselves call job candidates on pre-screening calls. They hire an external recruiter, a staffing agency, or an interview-screening company to pre-screen job applicants.

Employers give these service-providers scripts from which to read and questions to ask that will filter out most of the candidates. If you think you are being interviewed by one of these service-providers, you need to restrict your answers to the questions asked. In other words, don't attempt to build a relationship or have a "conversation" with these paid screeners.

To a pre-screening service-provider, you are just one faceless voice among many. You can't ask detailed questions about the job because these screeners have no knowledge of the job other than the script they were given. Your goal should be to answer their questions so you can advance to an in-person interview with the person who has the power to hire you.

Whether an employer outsources the pre-screening process to an external service provider or not, the pre-screening is usually broken into two stages. One with general employment-type questions and another with job-specific questions. In the first stage, you are asked basic questions about your employability. These questions include:

- Are you interested in the job?
- Are you available to work?
- Do you have visible tattoos?
- Can you work the shifts required? (1st, 2nd, graveyard, etc.)
- Are you available for business travel? How often?
- Are you within a reasonable commuting distance to the office?
- Do you have a reliable means of transportation to get to work on time?
- What is your desired salary?

These are the "must-pass" questions of a pre-screening call. You basically must answer, "Yes" to all of them, and be within the company's pay range to move to the next stage of the hiring process. If you answer, "No" to any of these, you will likely be filtered out and your candidacy will end.

The standard questions are not difficult. Most of them require short answers. Some of them, like business travel, are a little less definite. Since business travel fluctuates, the employer may be flexible or will ask for broad answers. But if the job requires that you work 2nd shift, it's unlikely you will move onto the in-person interview if you cannot work that shift.

The second pre-screening stage is job-specific. It consists of two broad categories of questions relative to performing the job:

- Behavioral questions that delve into how you work with other people

- Technical questions that ask about your knowledge of the job

Behavioral questions tell the interviewer how you behaved in the past in a specific situation the interviewer poses – a situation that is likely to occur on the job. The theory is that past behavior predicts future behavior. The most common behavioral questions are:

- Describe a stressful work situation and how you overcame it.

- Describe a time when you had to deal with a difficult person. What was the outcome?

- Describe a time when a deadline was pushed forward. How did you meet the new deadline?

- Describe a time when you developed a new process or improved an existing process.

- Describe a time when you were creative in a work situation.

Situational interview questions are a type of behavioral questions, but they deal with hypothetical behavior rather than past behavior. They should be answered, however, in the behavioral fashion. You should answer these questions in a structured manner that is based on a cause-context-result format. That is, describe the problem, say, working with a difficult person. Then set the context such as a fast approaching deadline. Finally, end with the result. For instance, you could say that you met the deadline by listening to and empathizing with a difficult worker, allowing both of you to meet the deadline.

Behavioral and situational interview questions are meant to filter out job candidates who cannot deal with common work situations in the manner desired by the employer. This is important nowadays because much work today is team-based and project-driven.

The other type of job-specific pre-screening is technical. Here, for example, are a few pre-screening questions for a UNIX Administrator: What is SNA? What is PAM? If you have heard of PAM, state why it is useful? What is DHCP? Can you give me an example of how DHCP is used? What file do you set up on a machine to make it use DNS?

Before we move onto the other types of pre-screening formats, let's revisit the issue of phone communication skills. As stated before, most people believe that the primary reason why job candidates do not move out of the pre-screening stage and into the interviewing stage is a lack of phone skills. So, they give job candidates mock interviews in the belief that "practice makes perfect."

Mock interviews can be useful. They can force a candidate to really answer questions they are likely to be asked. But the average candidate does not need mock interview practice to receive invitations for in-person interviews. Most people can answer the typical questions and draw on their experience to give at least an acceptable answer to the hard questions.

So, if phone skills are not a big problem for most people, what is? The answer is having the ability to *read* the pre-screening call in its proper context.

A phone screen is usually the beginning of the pre-screening process rather than the end of it. Phone screeners can be anyone from a junior staff member with a list of questions to highly experienced executive recruiters who know exactly what the employer is looking for. How you field a phone screening call depends on understanding whom you are talking to and what is their interest (or standing) in the hiring decision. A typical phone screener from a staffing agency has no vested interest in whether you are interviewed, hired, or rejected. So doing anything that is beyond the limited scope of the screener will kill your chances of moving forward in the hiring process.

Conversely, if you are talking to a savvy recruiter who has a direct relationship with the employer and is likely to get a hefty commission on your placement (hiring), then you must build a relationship with the recruiter and project yourself as savvy, experienced and sharp so the recruiter feels comfortable passing you on to the client.

Tips on Other Pre-Screening Mechanisms

Employers now use three other types of pre-screening mechanisms to gain information about a job candidate before inviting someone to an in-person interview. They are:

- Skype interviews
- Audio recordings
- Video recordings
- Meet-and-greet interviews

Skype interviews allow the employer to see the interviewee while asking the pre-screening questions. Skype interviews tell more about a candidate than a phone interview. You will need a computer equipped with a webcam, a high-speed Internet connection, and a Skype account.

Treat a Skype interview like an in-person interview. Dress up in interview attire and ensure the background is white or neutral with no distractions for the interviewer. Arrange for noisy pets or children to be elsewhere during the interview. Get used to the technology prior to the interview. Ensure your computer is at eye level with the camera so you are not looking up, which is usually unflattering. Test your setup in advance to adjust video exposure, white balance, etc. This is especially important for out-of-area job candidates, since Skype interviews are often replacing in-person interviews.

Audio and video recordings are short media segments (45 seconds to 2 minutes) in which a candidate answers a question posed by the interviewer. You need to be able to create these media types to answer these questions. You should write a short script prior to making the recording. Remember, it doesn't take many words to produce a 45-second audio or video. So be concise and "on point" when you create audio files. Here are some sample questions:

- In two minutes, tell us who you are.

- In one minute, tell us if you have ever led a team and what you were able to accomplish.

- Discuss a detailed example of your IT capabilities.

Meet-and-greet interviews occur when an employer calls and then invites you to his office or a coffee shop for an informal chat. But during this "interview" no questions are asked. No application form is completed. The employer is checking you out and trying to determine what he wants. Be pleasant yet cautious during this type of interview. Ask questions to pin down when he is going to hire someone. If you can't, then this employer may not be hiring at all. He may be trying to figure out something only he knows.

7. How to Solve a "No Job Offer" Problem

If you are invited to an employer's office for an in-person interview, congratulations! You are now one of the finalists and near the end of a long job search campaign. This is no small accomplishment. Due to online recruitment, it is common to compete against 200 or more job applicants. No matter what the size of the initial group of candidates, it was narrowed down to about five candidates (which now includes you) who have been invited to the employer's office for an in-person interview. One candidate of this small group will get a job offer.

But what happens if you are one of the five candidates who are interviewed yet don't get the job offer? To overcome this problem, let's discuss the intrinsic nature of hiring decisions to better understand what kind of "war" you are waging.

How Hiring Decisions Are Made

Hiring decisions are filled with contradictions. Understanding these contradictions is the first step in solving a "No Job Offer" problem. In general, a hiring decision is based upon a variety of factors that determine in the employer's mind which of the five finalists is the "best fit" for the job. They want the candidate who not only has the skills, but also would easily "fit" into the current team with little or no training.

Training is a big deal for employers today. They prefer not to hire anyone who needs training. Why? At face value, it's about money. Why should employers pay to train employees if they can use online recruitment to find qualified job candidates who are immediately ready to contribute to the company's bottomline?

Beyond the need for the right "fit," there may be another reason why one finalist gets a job offer and the others do not. This has to do with the established relationship one candidate has that others do not. In this regard, applicants fall into one of three categories:

- Internal candidate (currently works for the employer)
- Employee referral (candidate personally knows a current employee)
- External candidate (no relationship to the employer)

Competing against an internal candidate is the most common reason a job candidate "finalist" doesn't get hired quickly. Internal candidates already have a relationship with the employer so they have a documented track record of their performance, work ethic, personality traits, and likeability. This is why the internal candidate is usually the most frequent "new" hire.

Even knowing a current employee makes a big difference – a referred candidate is usually preferred over an external candidate. This is why external candidates are at a disadvantage even when they are as qualified as any of the other finalists. If an employer doesn't know the external candidate, he really doesn't know if the candidate will fit into the current work team.

One of the fears that employers have is hiring someone who isn't the "right fit." If they hire someone who does not work out, it can send shockwaves throughout a work team and may precipitate a mass exodus of critical team members. The best way to deal with being an external candidate is to find contacts within the company and get an employee referral; this alone will improve your chances of getting a job offer.

Beyond the bias of existing relationships in hiring decisions, the core reason one finalist is hired and another is not is pure competitiveness. Let's discuss the term "competitiveness" for a moment.

"Competitiveness" has a number of definitions. In the hiring process, it is used to refer primarily to wages, as in: "I can give you a competitive salary." But today, the term has a much broader meaning. Competitiveness now relates to the mixture of salary, qualifications, and intangibles such as the right "cultural fit."

In addition, when junior staff members are invited to "team-interview" a finalist, one can almost guarantee that their decision will depend on their subjective feeling regarding which candidate they would most like to work with. When team-interviewing was first introduced, it was an effective way to spread the risk of hiring decisions. Involving employees at the department or team level was a way to ensure the new hire would be a good fit with the existing team. It took the hiring decision out of the hands of a few higher-ups in the organization. However, team interviews seem to have morphed into popularity contests. Nonetheless, team interviewing remains popular among employers.

Why You Didn't Get Hired Quickly

If you are not competitive enough to win the job for which you have interviewed, you may be able to trace the source of the problem back to the initial phase of your job search. If you apply to jobs for which you are not fully qualified, you may able to win an interview, but a lack of competitiveness will kill your candidacy.

Improper selection of a job ad can occur when you have a vague objective. As stated earlier, since employers use complex targeting techniques to identify job candidates, they are looking for near-perfect matches. If you do not fit their idea of the perfect candidate, you may be able to snag an in-person interview, but not be the one who wins the job.

A further cause of a competitiveness problem is the type of job campaign you are waging. There are three types of job search campaigns:

- Positional
- Industry Change
- Combination (Positional + Industry Change)

A positional campaign is a career transition from one type of job and industry to a similar job and industry. This type of campaign is commonly called a "lateral" career change and places you in the most desirable competitive position.

An industry change campaign is a career transition from the same type of job, but for a different industry. This type places you at a disadvantage when you are competing against finalists who already have industry experience especially with notable, highly branded companies.

A combination campaign is a career transition from one job type *and* industry to another job type *and* industry. This type of campaign makes you the least competitive because you are competing against interview finalists who both job title and industry experience.

Be mindful of what kind of job campaign you are waging. If you do not get a job offer, you may want to stick with a positional job campaign in order to improve your competitiveness. In addition to considering the type of job search campaign you will launch, you should also consider how well you meet the employer's needs regarding the following four factors:

- Industry work experience (in companies similar to the employer)
- Career level (entry, experienced non-manager, staff manager, senior manager, executive)
- Portfolio of accomplishments (tangible proof of skills)
- Money (affordability: within the employer's range)

In your post-interview analysis, spend some time reviewing the job ad again. Determine how you measure up in terms of the company's industry and business line. You will improve your chances for a job offer if you meet the job's requirements as close as possible.

If you find that the brunt of your experience is in different kinds of companies or business lines, it may be time to seek out companies looking for skills closer to your overall experience if you are not getting a job offer. You may have to experiment a few times to see what works for you. But if you are regularly getting in-person interviews, you are close to a job offer. How you do at making the necessary adjustments to your job search will be what brings you to the winner's circle.

8. How to Restart a Job Search on a Winning Path

Recognizing your job search isn't performing adequately is the first step in the process of getting it back on track again. The first telltale sign of a failing job search is a lack of recruiter inquiries or in-person interviews. A job search stretched out to over 6 months or more is another sign of a problem. Often the best way to correct a problematic job search is to restart your search with a fresh approach. This chapter will tell you how to do it.

When most people restart their job searches, they go back and take a look at their résumé to see how it can be improved. But a résumé rewrite should not be the first place to restart a job search.

The first action you should take in restarting your job search is to leverage your current and past work relationships to help you get hired. This is how you should begin:

List your family members who can help you directly or indirectly help you find a job:

1. _____
2. _____
3. _____
4. _____
5. _____

List your friends who can directly or indirectly help you find a job:

1. _____
2. _____
3. _____
4. _____
5. _____

List your ex-bosses/co-workers who can directly or indirectly help you find a job:

1. _____
2. _____
3. _____
4. _____

5. _____

List the people in your church, personal, social, professional or athletic clubs you know who can directly or indirectly help you find a job:

1. _____

2. _____

3. _____

4. _____

5. _____

List your neighbors/acquaintances who can directly or indirectly help you find a job:

1. _____

2. _____

3. _____

4. _____

5. _____

Completing these five lists usually generates at least five people each. So, by taking one hour to formulate these lists, you can get about 25 people who can directly or indirectly help you get a job.

You then want to contact these people (e.g. in person, phone, email, etc.) and reconnect with them. As you reconnect, at the appropriate moment in your conversation, ask them if they know of any companies that are hiring. If they are working for one of these companies, ask them if they can give you a referral. Apply for the job and make sure you insert your referral's name in the appropriate section of the application form. This will tag your job application as a "referred" applicant, which will give you preference over external candidates who search the Internet and apply for jobs through job boards, job ad aggregators or social recruiting sites.

Successful job seeking is primarily a relationship-building task. Real relationships in your personal life will always reap more job leads than virtual relationships developed via the Internet. Virtual relationships don't hurt, but for **most** of the millions in the U.S. who are actively searching for a job, they will not provide the key relationships needed to get hired.

9. Résumés that Rank High in Database Searches

There are many different ways to write a résumé. Unfortunately, most of them do not obtain recruiter inquiries when used in an online job application or on résumé posting site because they do not obtain high ranking in database searches.

To obtain high ranking, a résumé must be written for a database. It will be very dense with information to increase the "keyword population" of the résumé. The keyword population is the number of noun-based, job-specific keywords per page. When a résumé contains lots of keywords, the résumé search engine software has enough data to judge its merits and rank your résumé higher than other résumés in the database.

A high-ranking résumé will also repeat keywords to not only increase the number of keywords in the résumé, but also to compensate for those recruiters who skim résumés in just a few seconds. Additionally, a high-ranking résumé also has a large number of technical skill keywords. Technical keywords are the most popular keywords used by recruiters to find job candidates.

There is little mention of "people skills" and no use of clichéd language (e.g., team player, etc.). These traits are considered later, usually during an in-person interview, when behavioral questions are asked.

In the job history section, the job experience is spread over a series of sub-heads, which are also keywords. This technique not only increases the keyword density, but also makes it more skimmable for human reviewers.

In addition, the job narratives are written differently. Instead of the short phrases used in a traditional résumé, the descriptions in a high-ranking online résumé are described in detail using pertinent keywords. It may seem you are overwriting the job descriptions. In some respects, you are. But you do it to overcompensate for the increased competition that occurs during résumé database searches.

This is an example of a résumé that frequently received high ranking in database searches because it is rich in keywords and has very detailed descriptions of tasks, skills and accomplishments:

CAREER PROFILE

Digital marketing professional with experience in roles as varied as Content Strategist, Interactive Copywriter, Digital Project Coordinator, Social Media Specialist and Web Analyst.

SUMMARY OF QUALIFICATIONS

Five years experience in website project management, content management & development, maintenance and administration and integrated marketing experience, spanning market strategy development from conception to deployment, media buying/purchasing ad space, creating banner ads and landing pages in an agency and corporate setting.

TECHNICAL COMPETENCIES

HTML, CSS, SEO, SEM, Google Analytics, WordPress, Drupal, Visio, Arc View 10, C++, SQL, Constant Contact, Dreamweaver, Illustrator, Photoshop, MS Office, Word, Excel, Access, PowerPoint

PROFESSIONAL EXPERIENCE

Digital Project Manager / Interactive Copywriter, ABC Ad Agency, Chicago, IL. 6/2011 – Present.

- **Project Management**: Manage project team including writers, developers, and graphic designers to deliver a product that's within guidelines. Oversee the writing and editing of client marketing communications. Liaise with clients to ensure the proper delivery of approved marketing strategies and deliverables. Coach team members when necessary. Maintain process workflows.

- **Marketing Strategy**: Participate in all areas from marketing strategy development, from conception to deployment. Customize marketing strategies, perform initial research, engage in outreach initiatives, establish project timelines, and content development. Develop and implement web strategies for improved user experience, usability, SEO, marketing, and functionality. Work collaboratively across the company to determine web and content needs, potential content sources and customer-focused solutions.

- **Web Content Management**: Manage, direct and facilitate the flow of content to website(s) through collaboration with other content contributors. Providing basic training for new content contributors. Implement content updates across public and internal web sites. Apply and maintain quality assurance standards for copy and media management.

- **Content Production**: Write and copy edit interactive and print projects including website content, email blasts, brochures, advertisements, and brand strategy.

- **Client Service**: Liaise with clients to ensure the proper delivery of approved marketing strategies and deliverables. Improve client service by emphasizing communication on a regular basis and by completing marketing material projects prior to deadline.

- **Social Media**: Implement social media strategies on interactive platforms (WordPress, Tumblr, YouTube, Facebook, Twitter, LinkedIn and FourSquare). Assist team in managing communities and supporting social media strategies.

Communications Coordinator, DEF Company, Des Moines, IA. 4/2010 – 5/2011.

- **Project Management**: Functioned as a project manager charged with developing relationships with external contributors (e.g., student, professors, and community members) by coordinating in-person meetings to encourage and ensure that communications were consistent with University strategy and communicated a positive, student-oriented style.

- **Web Analytics**: Drafted web analytics reports to measure success of SEO initiatives.

- **Content Management**: Edited University web content using Word Press and Dreamweaver.

- **Social Media**: Grew social media membership via Facebook, Twitter and Foursquare by 64% as measured through Google Analytics.

Writer/Editor, GHI Magazine, New York, NY. 10/2009 – 12/2010

- **Writing**: Wrote bi-weekly reviews for newly released movies with 35 published reviews.

- **Public Relations**: Conducted interviews with nationally recognized and local filmmaker guests at annual film events, such as the Art Film Festival, and wrote magazine articles to publicize the events and promote the cultural scene.

- Web Content Manager, XYX Company, Houston, TX. 1/2008 – 10/2009

- **Content Production**: Responsible for content production by adding new content and enhancing articles with photos, background articles, related links to other websites and multimedia material.

- **Writing & Editing**: Copyedited and proofread informational and instructional accessibility web content submitted by subject matter experts, ensuring all publications were error-free and content was optimized for the targeted audience.

- **Web Design**: Designed and maintained web pages with HTML and Dreamweaver. Collaborated with users to determine requirements and security needs; developed and presented initial design ideas and associated tools.

- **Web Quality Assurance**: Tested functionality to ensure objectives were achieved. Improved website quality by proofreading content and HTML coding.

EDUCATION

- B.A. Degree in English, University of Michigan– 3.46/4.0 GPA 9/2004– 5/2011.

10. The Only Cover Letters You'll Ever Need

Most cover letters don't get read because they appear to be *lifted* from the Internet. Those blunt words are meant to highlight an important point. Most cover letters are carbon copies of letters used over and over by a countless number of job seekers. The important point is this: if you are a carbon copy of every other job candidate, why should a recruiter take a closer look at you? If you write a letter that stands out from the others, you have a better chance of moving forward in the hiring process.

A cover letter that does not tell a recruiter why you should be hired over all other candidates should not accompany a job application. Poor cover letters do not persuade. They may even be a detriment to your job candidacy.

Here is an example of a letter that will **not** get you a call:

Dear Hiring Manager,

I am deeply motivated to obtain a position where I can leverage my dynamic education and previous experience to develop innovative solutions and support market growth within a quality-oriented business culture that holds long-term vision. In pursuit of continued professional challenges, please accept this application for the Assistant Logistics Manager. I believe this position will provide me with a unique opportunity to maximize my professional potential with emphasis on team collaboration, leadership, and exposure to numerous crucial areas within this discipline. Paired with your commitment to sustainability and philanthropy, this position is a strong match with my professional aspirations and core personal values.

The snapshot below outlines my key competencies and attributes, keenly matched with your needs:

- *Qualifying Education & Experience: Currently completing final semester leading to a Bachelor of Science degree with majors in International Business Management and Economics from ABC College. Successfully completed dynamic Collaborative Planning, Forecasting, and Replenishment Internship at DEF Corporation within a cross-functional team driven environment. .*

- *Demonstrated Leadership: Has continuously and enthusiastically stepped into strategic leadership roles across collegiate and professional tenure. Collegiate roles include, but are not limited to, Founder (2010-Present) of a public LLP investment organization and Orientation Leader (2009-Present).*

- *Effective Communication, Relationship Management, & Collaborative Approach: Demonstrated ability to confidently engage, persuade, and foster lasting relationships with colleagues and partners; exceptional command of written and spoken communication leading to efficient information procurement and effective relationship development; works collaboratively with managers, colleagues, and key third party players.*

- *Personal Attributes: Change agent, innovative, analytical, critical thinking, data-driven, results-oriented, flexible, ambitious, organized, diplomatic, and enterprising.*

The details above are just a brief preview of my skills and accomplishments; I urge you to fully review my resume, which details the wide range of experiential and educational training. I would appreciate an opportunity to meet with you to further discuss how my experience will best fulfill your needs for this position. Please call me at 123.456.7890 or email me at name@name.com to schedule an interview.

The problem with the above letter is that it's boring, wordy, jargonistic, sterile, and impersonal. A good cover letter should tell a story. It should be personal, authentic, and real. The following letter is a rewrite of the original cover letter:

Dear Hiring Manager,

Your job posting for an Assistant Logistics Manager (REQ# F4579) caught my interest because the skills you desire dovetail perfectly with my experience in logistics solutions, forecasting, replenishment, and project management.

I have a Bachelors degree in International Business Management and offer specialized experience in areas directly relevant to this position such as Collaborative Planning, Forecasting, and Replenishment. I believe I am the perfect choice for you to efficiently manage its inventory, fulfillment, and planning functions.

In brief, I am an entrepreneurial, action-oriented individual who can accomplish goals from start to finish. In my most recent position at Kellogg Company (NYSE: K), I co-managed national supply SKUs across two departments, consisting of a product portfolio totaling $225M+ in gross sales. I also provided analysis to the customer team management by supporting business planning and execution through accurate forecasting.

Here is what I offer you:

- *Expertise in collaborative demand planning of product portfolios over the entire product life cycle.*
- *Ability to effectively collaborate in highly matrixed organization within the Planning, Purchasing, and Sales disciplines.*
- *Adept at building rapport with diverse audiences and cultivating mutually beneficial relationships with colleagues, clients, and partners.*
- *High level of proficiency in SAP, MS Office Suite, featuring advanced Excel skills.*

I have a unique balance between business acumen and technical finesse that I believe would be useful to this position. I have managed service and inventory levels for the entirety of the corporation's Supply Chain, influencing item forecast recommendations for optimal inventory levels, including the spearheading of projects that improved efficiency and reduced replenishment costs.

As a problem solver and relationship builder, I'm known for my ability to turn ideas into actionable programs. Helping companies understand how to manage their product portfolios is a particular skill of mine. This is increasingly important at a time when resource allocation and inventory control have a highly visible and heightened impact to the corporate balance sheet.

I would appreciate the opportunity to meet with you to discuss this position. I can be contacted by phone at (123) 456-7890, or by email at name@name.com.

The above letter is shorter and says more about the job seeker and his knowledge, skills and abilities. The reader becomes interested in the job seeker because he comes off as intelligent and interesting. While this letter focuses on the job seeker's skills, it can be rewritten to emphasize his achievements as well. The following letter emphasizes the job seeker's achievements:

Dear Hiring Manager,

Please accept the enclosed résumé for consideration for the position of Business Management Analyst (Job Number: GG89). I am currently seeking employment with a consulting firm serving the Fortune 500 corporate community where the need of a business management champion who also has knowledge, skills, and abilities in process optimization and lean techniques is critical.

In brief, I am an entrepreneurial individual with superb client service skills who can accomplish goals from start to finish. In my most recent position at Kellogg Company (NYSE: K), I co-managed national supply SKUs across two departments, consisting of a product portfolio totaling $225M+ in gross sales. I also was a member of a project team that facilitated business process optimization to improve relationships with downstream partners.

Here is a sample of the value I can bring to your business strategy consulting team:

- *Business Process Redesign: After the stand-alone reporting system went down, I swiftly learned the new system and readapted all 12 reports to the new online system. This allowed the logistics team to continue their departmental reporting without skipping a beat.*

- *Data Analysis Consulting: Drove accurate forecasting by analyzing trending metrics (quantitative) and collaborating with Retail Supply Chain partners (qualitative) to further uncover, develop, communicate, and implement change to drive positive results for departmental ownership.*

- *Business Process Documentation: Using lean techniques, I implemented a process improvement consisting of a report that had visibility for the entire team (Sales + Logistics) - VP to the analyst level. I was able to save 1,560 annual man-hours through the implementation of a VBA macro.*

I have a unique balance between business acumen and technical finesse that I believe would be useful to in this position. I am a pro-active problem solver with a team-oriented style who has an innate ability to turn ideas into initiatives that answer the needs of clients. With a Bachelors degree in International Business Management and specialized experience in areas directly relevant to this position, I believe I am the perfect choice for XYZ Consulting to provide business process consulting to its valued clients.

I would appreciate the opportunity to meet with you to discuss this contract. I can be contacted by phone at (123) 456-7890, or by email at name@name.com.

If you feel you should emphasize your skills in a job application, use the former letter. But if you feel you should emphasize your achievements, use the latter letter. The one you choose will depend on the needs of the employer. In the end, these are the only cover letters you'll ever need.

11. How to Run a Successful Job Search

At some point, you will move your job search from obtaining personal referrals to applying to jobs using online job portals such as job boards and social recruiting sites. This move is so common (even career counselors suggest it) that most people have no doubt they will find a job this way. Unfortunately, the hiring success rates of job boards and social recruiting sites can be misleading despite widely held beliefs to the contrary.

As previously stated in this book, millions of job seekers use online job portals and social recruiting sites to run their job search campaigns and do not get hired because of the high level of competition these sites create in an economy that isn't driving enough job creation to employ everyone seeking a job through these sites.

Keep in mind that most people have a hard enough time winning a job when they are competing against a mere 10 candidates. Place them in a pool of 100, 1000 or 10,000 candidates and it becomes next to impossible for the typical worker to get hired unless they are the perfect job candidate in all respects – someone who has demonstrated record of performing all job tasks described in a job ad and is the "ideal" cultural fit for the organization.

Despite the competition, you can get hired through online job portals. You just need to use them in such a way so the odds are not against you. Here's how to do it:

Work with Employers, Not the Gatekeepers

It is important to understand that online job portals are the middlemen or gatekeepers of the hiring process. They insert themselves between you, the job seeker, and the employer. While online job portals are free to use, you do pay a price. When you provide your career data to online job portals, they turn around and provide it employers in the form of large, résumé databases, which increase competition between you and other job seekers. The best thing you can do is to eliminate these gatekeepers from your job search and work directly with employers. This will speed up your hiring process, take less of your time, and decrease your job competition.

Determine Your Industry Sector

As previously stated, industry experience has risen to a new level of importance since online recruitment was introduced. Because it gives a business context to your job skills, employers search for job candidates with industry experience to obtain candidates who are more likely to be best-fit employees. Knowing your industry will ensure that you are considering employment at companies that are likely to value your experience.

In general, there are 16 major industry sectors in the U.S. economy. They are:

- Agriculture
- Construction
- Consumer Packaged Goods
- Defense
- Education
- Energy
- Finance
- Government
- Healthcare
- Hospitality
- Industrial
- Information Technology
- Manufacturing
- Mining
- Transportation
- Utilities

Each of these industry sectors consists of many different companies, all of which are likely to have similar businesses, work cultures and needs for employees with industry-sensitive skills.

Select Your Preferred Employers

Once you know your industry sector, use your favorite Web search engine to find the companies within your industry sector. Use the keywords **name of industry + company list** to find them. You will then have formed a list of your preferred employers. For instance, in the consumer packaged goods industry, these are some of the top companies:

- Procter & Gamble
- Pfizer

- Unilever
- L'Oreal
- Kimberly-Clark
- Johnson & Johnson
- Avon Products
- Henkel
- Nestle
- Clorox
- Bausch & Lomb
- Limited Brands

Visit Your Preferred Employers' Corporate Career Sites

Instead of searching for jobs on public job boards, job-ad aggregator sites or social media recruiting sites get in the habit of visiting your preferred companies' websites first. Search for **local** jobs posted in their career sites. Use keywords that describe your skills to find the jobs for which you are qualified. Record the names of the job titles. Ensure your résumé is aligned to the skills and experience desired in the job ads, then do the following:

Set Up Job Alerts

Create job alerts, described by the job titles you found. The career site software will automatically send job openings to you via email when they are posted on an employer's website. Job alerts replace all the searching for jobs on job boards and social recruiting sites. This approach will save you a lot of time and make you more responsive to job openings.

Post Your Résumé

Next, create a profile on the employer's site and post your résumé. This will also help you save time because you will have your résumé ready-to-go at the employer's site. Write a relevant cover letter, upload it to the job application, and then apply for the job.

Continue to Build Your Preferred Employer List

Beyond the initial set up of job alerts and profiles on the employers' career sites, you should spend an hour or so once a week looking for more companies in your industry sector. Repeat the same process outlined above. Instead of posting your résumé to job boards, you will be providing it directly to employers – not gatekeepers to pass onto employers. Once again, this approach eliminates the middlemen (job boards and social recruiting sites) and other gatekeepers from your job search. It allows you to respond more quickly to an employer's new job openings.

Resources for Finding Companies by Industry Sector

To find the complete lists of hundreds of companies by industry sector, you can search via a web search engine using "company list + name of industry," or you can go to the following information sources:

Yahoo! Industry Center: https://biz.yahoo.com/p/sum_conameu.html

Bloomberg: https://biz.yahoo.com/p/sum_conameu.html

Fortune 500: http://fortune.com/fortune500/

Note: Website hyperlinks often change. If the above links do not work, then go to your favorite Web Search Engine, and search for companies using the following keywords: *Fortune 500 + Company List*.

Glossary

Online Recruitment: any Internet-enabled intermediary between an individual job seeker and an employer. It can include: email; job boards; recruiting agency websites; staffing firm websites; newspaper classified websites; governmental career (workforce development) websites; corporate career sites; social media recruiting sites; professional association websites; industry newsletters and blogs.

Job Board: the informal name applied to a website that contains databases of résumés and job ads. Job seekers search the job ad database for current openings, while employers or recruiters search the résumé database for job candidates to interview.

Job Title Experience: the term that applies to a job you have actually held. For example, if you have held the position of Office Manager or Electronic Service Technician, then these are your job title experiences. Job title experience does not apply to transferable skills you have acquired in a similar job that would make you qualified for the position of Office Manager or Electronic Service Technician. Job title experience is very important with respect to how résumés get ranked in database searches. For example, if your most recent position was Office Manager and a recruiter was searching for an office manager, your job title experience would rank you very high in a database search. Conversely, if you are currently a military veteran who was recently a First Sergeant, functioning as a personnel manager, and you applied for a Human Resources Manager job, you could very well have the (transferable) skills to perform the HR job, but since you have never actually held an HR Manager's job, you do not have job title experience and your résumé would rank much lower in résumé database searches. A lack of job title experience can cause a "No Calls" problem.

Social Recruiting Sites: the name applied to websites that use social media for finding job candidates. Similar to job boards, they contain candidate profiles and résumés, as well as job ads. Recruiters primarily use social recruiting sites to search for candidates by keywords. They also use them to learn more about a candidate, basically, as an informal background check. The important difference between a job board and a social recruiting site is that members of social recruiting sites can connect with other members. This networking *may* generate additional referrals or job leads.

Recruiter: a sales person or representative, who is usually compensated by employers, and acts as a "gatekeeper" in the hiring process. There are different types of recruiters. Executive recruiters or "headhunters" are the most well known. They work with high-wage job seekers and obtain large commissions when they place an executive with an employer. Technical recruiters work with technical-skilled job seekers and perform a role similar to that of an executive recruiter. Some recruiters work for staffing agencies; these people are on salary and generally do not earn large commissions. Instead, they work on behalf of their client, the employer, to find appropriate job candidates. Offshore recruiters are the newest type of recruiter. They work for companies based outside of the U.S. who are seeking U.S. workers to fill their positions based in the U.S. They exist primarily due to the limitations the U.S. government places on guest worker visas, such as H1-bs.

Sourcing: all actions taken by both recruiters and hiring managers to find people for open positions. Sourcing is synonymous with "selecting" or "finding." In the past, recruiters and hiring managers used contacts they had developed through networked "human relationships" to source candidates. Nowadays, recruiters usually source candidates by using keyword searches of résumé databases.

Résumé Database: a "digital warehouse" of career information of both active and passive job candidates. These databases can contain 300 million résumés or more.

Online Résumé: a résumé written specifically for a résumé database. It emphasizes information and keywords over visual format. These résumés are much longer than the traditional one-page résumé. In theory, they are limitless since the length of a résumé does not really matter for a database; however, most online résumés are two to four pages in length.

Résumé Visibility: the term that describes when a résumé obtains high ranking in résumé database searches. High ranking equals high visibility, which translates into frequent callbacks by recruiters who view the résumé in an online recruitment database.

Executive Résumé Sample

Versatile and results-driven, community-oriented leader who's able to leverage marketing, public relations, event planning, volunteer & nonprofit management, and business development expertise to benefit the strategies, growth, development and stability of a nonprofit organization.

- **Profile**: Well-rounded nonprofit executive with ten years of experience and a proven record in fostering goodwill, generating constituent support and inspiring loyalty in local communities by consistently building relationships with stakeholders to support agency initiatives.

- **Volunteer Recruitment Leadership**: Team leader in the organization's legislative efforts including recruiting volunteers to participate in grassroots efforts to ensure the 2006 Tobacco Tax Initiative qualified for the ballot.

- **Exceeded Fundraising Targets**: Led the Relay for Life of Madison raising $30,000, twice the event goal. Led four communities in raising $320,000 for cancer research.

PROFESSIONAL EXPERIENCE

Regional Development Manager, Company ABC, San Francisco, CA
June 2012—Nov 2012

- **Fundraising**: Contributed to the fundraising goals of Company ABC by managing all efforts to raise funds through Company ABC's Walks, exceeding fundraising goal by 150%. Managed events and relationships in California, Georgia, Alabama, Arizona and Utah.

- **Event Management**: Held all event planning responsibilities including identifying locations, developing event budgets, risk management, vendor management and contracting for walks, dodge ball tournaments and endurance hikes

- **Corporate Relations**: Recruited companies throughout the western region to host Return to Recess and third party fundraisers in 2010. Established successful relationships with Microsoft, San Francisco Giants, Eventbrite, Next Space and other such companies.

- **Volunteer Recruitment**: Identified volunteer needs and recruited local families and civic and business leaders to support Company ABC as members of committees and day of volunteers.

Project Manager, Company DEF, Rialto, CA July 2011—April 2012

- **Marketing**: Oversaw a virtual team that implemented internet marketing campaigns, developed project plans and budgets, established milestones and tasks, designated campaign expenditures, organized projects using CRM software, delegated tasks, monitored and supported staff, estimated time and expenses for new business proposals and advised CEO on software that could improves efficiency.

Company Director, XYZ Company, San Francisco, CA Aug 2008—Jan 2009

- **Leadership**: Conceptualized the Youth League, a service-learning program that helped students complete community service in competing teams. Revived the AmeriCorps Vista program by recruiting and placing two AmeriCorps Vistas that successfully implemented the Youth League and We Connect program.

- **Brand Management**: Improved poor image of the organization by presenting to and consistently attending Youth and Family Master Plan meetings where community needs were identified.

- **Grants/Fundraising**: Established a Day of Service grant that provided $10,000 in funding, resources and technical support for nine service projects planned and coordinated by local nonprofits. Collaborated with the Grants Manager in securing grants from Boeing, Allstate, Quaker Oats, and Target over six months.

- **Corporate Alliances**: Developed an adopt-a-project initiative that resulted in FedEx employees donating and installing a 10-station computer lab in an at-risk community. Supervised staff in the planning and execution of a school renovation for Wells Fargo Corporation employees.

- **Media Relations**: Secured 25 media hits during six months of leadership, a 500% increase over the previous six months.

Director of Marketing, RST Company, San Francisco, CA, May 2006—Aug 2008

- **Marketing Wins**: Established an annual holiday advertising campaign that targeted business and political leaders. Changed the political leaders' belief that they lacked job opportunities for the disabled by distributing a monthly newsletter highlighting success stories, disseminating a weekly e-mail blast of available positions and hosting quarterly job development meetings with leadership staff.

- **Corporate Alliances**: Collaborated with Menasha Corporation to find, train and place six adults with developmental disabilities in jobs.
- **Brand Management**: Established brand standards and redesigned all marketing collateral within the set guidelines
- **Event Management**: Established a system for planning, budgeting and coordinating events for 1,000 guests. Awarded special recognition during accreditation for marketing efforts and a system created to guide and track job development efforts

Community Development Manager, American Cancer Society, Los Angeles, CA Sept 2004—May 2006

- **Fundraising**: Led the Relay for Life in raising $60,000, twice the event goal. Led six communities in raising $570,000 for cancer research and services during a 2-year period.
- **Volunteer Recruitment**: Encouraged support of the American Cancer Society's legislative efforts including recruiting volunteers to participate in grassroots efforts to ensure the 2006 Tobacco Tax Initiative qualified for the ballot and motivating people to travel to Washington, DC for a Relay for Life and congressional lobbying events during Celebration on the Hill.

Recruitment and Marketing Coordinator, MNO, Atlanta, GA June 2002—June 2004

- **Volunteer Recruitment**: Recruited and trained 400 volunteer tutors
- **Event Management**: Planned and executed an event for 1,800 school children to promote reading daily. Planned and co-hosted a telethon that produced 300 volunteers in two hours.
- **Public Relations**: Produced a PSA featuring a popular radio personality promoting volunteerism in schools.
- **Community Service Innovation**: Expanded the number of work-study volunteer partnerships from one to nine, resulting in a significant increase in retained school volunteers.

EDUCATION

XYZ University, Atlanta, GA, August 1994 - May 1999

- B.A. in Mass Media Arts/Public Relations Concentration

University of Nevada, September 2000 - May 2001

- Masters of Business Administration

TECHNICAL PROFICIENCIES

- Nonprofit Software: Kintera Sphere
- Graphic Design: In Design, GIMP, Photoshop, Illustrator, Scribus, Publisher, Paint
- Web Design: HTML, CSS, WordPress
- Public Relations Software: Cision, Vocus, Burrell Luce
- Social Media: Facebook, Twitter, FourSquare, NING, Tumblr, StumbleUpon, Google Plus, LinkedIn, Meet Up, Youtube, Vimeo, Flickr, Photobucket, Scribd, Reddit, Delicious, Digg, Slideshare

Marketing Résumé Sample

Award-winning, business technology influencer with broad strategic alliance, technology, corporate and solutions marketing background and compelling record of driving growth and expanding profitability.

CAREER SUMMARY

- **Profile**: Senior alliance marketing executive with over twenty years of experience in identifying, developing, and growing win-win, profitable partnerships with corporations, organizations, professional associations, business groups and industry partners in a professional business services environment.

- **Partner Marketing Leader**: Expert at forging new business relationships with alliance partners to gain consensus to develop and execute partnership strategies and marketing programs on a worldwide level to track progress and measure success.

- **Business Development**: Demonstrated record of deploying successful 'go to market' strategies and joint marketing initiatives and alliances with leading technology corporations, including Microsoft, Facebook, Cisco, IBM, and Mentor Graphics

- **Organizational Style**: A tenacious, high energy and dedicated manager with a comprehensive outlook who balances practical business acumen with a special creative drive to see beyond the norm to envision what is truly possible.

KEY ACHIEVEMENTS

- **Generated a $4M Pipeline**: Planned and executed a record-breaking webcast marketing campaign with XYZ Company that generated a $4 million pipeline.

- **Built a Successful Public/Private Partnership**: Initiated and secured the University of Illinois as a founding member for Company ABC's launch of Cybersecurity products and services.

- **Deployed a Sustainable Campaign Strategy**: Initiated and delivered a PR program to help organizations save time, money, and trees, through adopting best practice, sustainable uses for Office software.

- **Broke Lead Generation Records**: Generated over 8,000 qualified leads, topping records, from an integrated partner marketing campaign for KLM Corporation.

PROFESSIONAL EXPERIENCE

ABC Company, Atlanta, GA 2015-Present

Marketing Consultant

- Developed and executed Open Source 'go to market' initiatives with strategic alliances, including Facebook, SAP, and Allstate.
- Achieved a 64% response rate from a joint online and direct mail marketing campaign with Facebook.
- Managed tradeshow planning and execution for key industry events, including Cisco Live, IBM Share, IBM Edge, Dell World, and Linuxcon.

Northwest Community College, Stockton, WA 2013-2014

Faculty, Business Technology

- Taught for-credit classes in Business Technology and Microsoft Office Suite.

DEF Technologies, Portland, OR 2012-2013

Enterprise Solutions Marketing Manager

- Developed and executed solutions marketing and execution strategy.
- Delivered content, tools, sales enablement programs to launch new SoC products.

GHI Corporation, Bellevue, WA 2010-2012

Strategic Alliance Marketing Manager

- Managed and executed alliance marketing, lead generation, communications and programs with Unified Communications and alliance partners including Microsoft, Cisco, Facebook, and Intel.

XYZ Corporation, Seattle, WA 2004-2009

Product Manager, 2006 – 2009

- Launched office product line in 20 industries and ten lines of business.
- Mitigated project risks to ensure customer satisfaction and complete 300 successful customer pilots.
- Produced over 152 customer case studies, 16 whitepapers, 15 Business Value Sales Kits, 8 customer videos, 20+ field, customer, and partner webcasts to launch Office and increase sales in 15 targeted markets.

- Identified and validated high-value markets and solutions. Designed and developed value propositions, messaging, use cases, processes, demos, collateral, tools, and training.
- Executed joint marketing campaigns with ISV partners to create awareness and generate leads.

Marketing Manager, 2004 – 2006

- Designed and executed initiative with 7 partners and 5 publishers to change chemical industry perception.
- Generated over 8,000 qualified leads, topping records, from an integrated partner marketing campaign.
- Attracted favorable media coverage in 200 sources including The Financial Times, Fortune, and Business Week.

Closed Solutions, Inc., Bellevue, WA 2001-2004

Channel Sales Executive

- Increased Microsoft partnership to Gold status and secured new alliances.
- Secured $4 million from alliances to fund technology and joint sales and marketing initiatives.

TECHNICAL SKILLS

Web Design, HTML/CSS, Adobe Creative Suite (Dreamweaver, Acrobat, Photoshop, Flash), Microsoft Office (Word, Excel, PowerPoint, OneNote, Outlook, Groove, SharePoint), Lotus Notes, Collaboration, Email, CRM, CMS, DBMS, SaaS, Cloud Computing, Salesforce, Relayware, Eloqua, Messaging & Communication apps

EDUCATION

MBA, Information Systems, Cornell University

PROFESSIONAL DEVELOPMENT

Certificate, Information Security and Risk Management, University of California, Seattle, WA

Military Résumé Sample

PROFILE

Results-oriented Site Manager with over 10 years of military contracting employment as a Linguist Site Manager, Assistant Site Manager, Transient Linguist Facility & Movement Manager, and Movement Control Specialist in Afghanistan, Iraq, Qatar, Egypt, UAE, Kuwait and Uzbekistan. Extensive experience liaising with the US Embassy and working with senior officers and representatives in both the civilian and military sectors. Direct knowledge and experience working with Local National Linguists. U.S Armed Forces veteran with 4 years of honorable military service in the fields of Logistics, Transportation and Movement Control during IOF/OEF campaigns.

COMPETENCIES

- Active Top Secret Clearance
- Project Management
- Strategic Planning
- Human Relations
- Logistics Coordination
- FOB Liaison
- Organizational Behavior
- Process Improvements
- Contract Administration

EXPERIENCE

Linguist Site Manager, ABC Company, Kabul Base Cluster, Afghanistan, 0y 8m, (Apr 2014 —Dec 2014)

- Oversee all functions associated with the operations, administration, logistics, safely, health and welfare and overall management of linguist programs within respective Area of Responsibility (AOR). Oversee site management team and all Local National Linguists. Assess operational processes and plans.
- Collaborated with linguist POCs to ensure linguist and military needs are addressed promptly.
- Rewarded employees with public recognition for performing their duties with excellence.

- Identified and corrected employee issues and concerns.
- Maintained accurate electronic records on employee status in the Personnel Tracking System (PTS) and the Military's secure Unit Linguist Manager's Database (ULMD).
- Successfully delivered movement reports, briefings, and other reports to senior management and military leaders.

Assistant Site Manager, ABC Company, Camp Las Vegas, Afghanistan, 0y 10m, (June 2013 —Apr 2014)

- Manage all categories of US Hire and all Local National Linguists and oversee all functions associated with the administration, logistics, safely, health and welfare and overall management of linguist programs within respective Area of Responsibility (AOR). Establish rapport with the military linguist POC's and BDOC.
- Earned Certificate of Excellence and Achievement for extraordinary results in retaining the linguist work force.
- Maintain 100% accountability of all assigned linguist personnel and equipment.
- Conduct recurring training to ensure compliance with company and DCAA guidance.
- Successfully completed the Annual Assessment and Annual Self-Assessment evaluations for all Staff and US
- Hire linguists in AOR and ensured the proper recognition of staff and linguists who excelled.
- Ensured participation and compliance with Quality Assurance/Quality Control programs.
- Achieved a 100% safety rating for deployed linguists.

Linguist Site Manager, DEF Company Baghdad, Iraq, 2y 6m, (June 2008—Dec 2010)

- Managed oversight of linguists POCs and performed translation request tracking, linguist assignment, and monitor prioritization. Administered linguist contracts regarding company policies, expectations, and benefits. Advised DRM, DD Operations, and Operations Manager of recurring or changing requirements.
- Achieved a 100% mission accomplishment rate with no loss of personnel, assets, or materials.

- Identified and corrected operational processes and plans, which resulted in faster, more accurate deployment of linguists to military units.

- Planned and seamlessly executed a monthly $200K local-national pay disbursement, by traveling to small patrol bases (PBs) and FOB's, resulting in a 100% completion rate over a 30-month period of time.

Movement Manager, GHI Company, Baghdad, Iraq, 0y 9m, (Oct 2007—June 2008)

- Supervised five TCN drivers and six US-hire theater movement support staff that provided support 24/7 by coordinating efficient transport of staff and linguists. Oversaw the execution and coordinated movement procedures within the entire AOR and 3rd country gateways.

- Earned "Logistician of the Month" Award for outstanding job performance in December 2007.

- Commended by the Chief of Staff for efficient movement of linguists.

Logistics Specialist, U.S. Army, Egypt, 4yr, (Aug 2000—Aug 2004)

- Coordinated transportation including, completing customer clearance waivers, cargo container inspections, and cargo documentation. Prepared OEF Custom Clearance Waivers to the United States Liaison Office in the U.S. embassy in Qatar informing them of arriving ships and requesting proper Arabic translated documents. Utilized the database Worldwide Port System (WPS) to pinpoint information ranging from estimated time arrival to ship voyage numbers.

- Created a new automated tracking system for container tracking to increase accuracy, accountability and decrease losses while working with MTMC in Doha, Qatar.

- Saved the U.S. government $100K by locating lost transport containers.

EDUCATION / TRAINING

- BS. Business Administration/Accounting, ABC University, Champaign, IL, USA.

- High School Diploma, St. John's High School, Milwaukee, WI, USA.

- U.S. Army Transportation School (12 weeks resident course), U.S. Military, Ft Eustis, USA, 23604.

- Worldwide Port Systems Course, (2 weeks resident course), U.S. Military, Ft Eustis, USA, 23604

- Basic Training (10 weeks resident course), U.S. Military, Ft. Sill, USA, 73503.

- GDSS (Global Decision Service System) (on the job training informal), U.S. Military, Afghanistan.

- GATES (Global Air Execution System) (on the job training, informal), U.S. Military, Afghanistan.

AWARDS

- Certificate of Excellence and Achievement

- Logistician of the Month Award

- Army Good Conduct Medal, 2004. Received Awards: 2 Army ARCOM, National Defense Service Medal, Army Service Ribbon, Global War on Terrorism Expeditionary Medal, Global War on Terrorism Service Medal.

New Graduate Résumé Sample 1

PROFILE

Award-winning, results-driven, and highly-organized Network Administrator who's accomplished in managing full network operations with the ability to diagnose problems and develop innovative solutions that are aligned to meet both customer and business needs. A skilled project leader capable of directing multiple tasks effectively with the ability to provide sound advice in the application of information management best practices. Professional manner and appearance. Excellent oral and written communication skills that emphasize consensus building. Able to perform work independently or in a team environment.

COMPETENCIES

- Professional Judgment
- Focused on Execution and Results
- Adaptability
- Influence Building Skills
- Customer Centered
- Continuous Improvement
- Ethics and Compliance
- Communicate Proactively

TECHNICAL PROFICIENCIES

- Platforms: Novell Netware 6.5 & Novell Clients, Apache webserver, Unix/Linux Administration, Software Wireless LAN, Open Source Security Administration, Active Directory, Symantec End Point Security, Microsoft Exchange 2003+ Server, SonicWall, Citrix, Windows Server 2003, Novell Open Enterprise Server, Novell GroupWise

- Languages: UNIX, HTML, XML, C++, JAVA, Python

- Productivity:Networking: MS Office Suite, MS Excel, MS PowerPoint, MS Project, MS Access, Past Perfect DB, MS Visio, LAN/WAN networking

- Digital Forensics: Tcp Dump, Wireshark, Snort, FTK imager, Forensics Tool Kit (FTK), Reg Ripper, Memoryze, PASCO, Switch

Port Analyzer (SPAN); retrieve information from networking equipment such as Routers, Switches and Firewalls for CAM table, ARP table, Logs and Access Control Lists; e-Discovery tasks such as evidence intake, chain of custody procedures, and forensic analysis

EDUCATION

- Master of Science Degree in Technology Studies, Information Assurance (GPA 3.83)– ABC University, 2012.
- Bachelor of Science Degree in Information Assurance (GPA 3.64) – ABC University, 2009. Dean's List Award, Winter Semester 2009.
- Associate in Applied Science Degree, Network Administration (GPA 3.73) – DEF College, 2007. Dean's List Award, Winter 08, Fall/08

CERTIFICATIONS

- Information Assurance Program, 2012
- SANS-FOR-408 (Compute Forensics Investigations), 2010.
- Cisco-Certified Network Associate (CCNA SECURITY) - ID CSCO 19029244, 2008.
- Novell Certified System Administrator (CAN) - ID OBEDTT5823, 2007.
- Security + Certified Professional - ID COMP001065319241, 2006.

PROFESSIONAL EXPERIENCE

Network Administrator, XYZ MUSEUM, Detroit, MI. 6/2010 – 6/2011.

- Skills Used: Windows server /Active Directory Management, Windows OS (XP, Vista, Win 7), Microsoft Office applications Linux Administration, Symantec End Point Security Rollout & Maintenance, Internal Network Auditing, Wireless Administration, Data Backup & Disaster Recovery, Network upgrade and maintenance, End User Support
- Responsible for the management and maintenance of a computer network consisting of 25 client machines (XP, vista, Win 7) along with a wireless network and network printers. Maintained information security oversight of all network systems.
- Configured new hardware, installed security software and corrected technical problems.
- Performed security vulnerability assessments and system configuration verifications.

- Conducted security scans of the installed software.

- Performed user support including, computer hardware, desktop applications, peripheral equipment.

- Reviewed existing security systems and identified discrepancies, security holes and risks.

- Implemented and enforced security policies, procedures and regulatory requirements.

- Introduced physical access control on the server and networking closet and configured/installed Symantec End Point Security on the server and clients. Enforced complex password policy via Win Server Group policy.

- Played a leadership role in advising and selecting network/IT procurement plans relative to budgetary constraints.

- Provided assistance in determining the usability of old network infrastructure and made recommendations on purchasing and replacing malfunctioning hardware.

ACHIEVEMENTS

- **Certificate of Appreciation**: for invaluable and proficient technical support as Network Administrator to correct a severely malfunctioning computer network where 3rd party support did not provide functional solutions. Upon correcting a range of network problems, the network returned to normal operation and did not experience any network outages. Result: Saved the Museum thousands of dollars in 3rd party support and equipment replacement costs.

New Graduate Résumé Sample 2

PROFILE

Detailed-oriented, organized and compassionate Registered Nurse, trained in patient-centered care, with demonstrated experience in project coordination, customer service and data entry. Honor Graduate of an NLNAC, accredited, School of Nursing. Clinical experience in medical/surgical, telemetry, obstetrics, pediatrics, mental health, and ICU. Ability to adapt in stressful situations. Strong interpersonal and communication skills. Enjoy working in a diverse work culture.

PRIMARY NURSING SKILLS

- Clinical/Physical Assessments
- Infection Control
- Asceptic Techniques
- Physiological Knowledge
- Administering Medication
- Medical Teamwork and Collaboration
- Health Promotion and Maintenance
- Communication & Listening

EDUCATIONAL BACKGROUND

Associate in Applied Science, Nursing – ABC College, May 2012. Cumulative GPA: 3.84/4.0.

- Licensure & Certification – RN LICENSE (IN PROGRESS). ANTICIPATED COMPLETION DATE: MAY 2012; CERTIFICATE OF ACHIEVEMENT IN PRACTICAL NURSING (LPN), AUG 2011; CPR, AMERICAN HEART ASSOCIATION, MAY 2010.

- Professional Development – MENTAL HEALTH FIRST AID. CONTINUING EDUCATION, ABC HOSPITAL (2012); THE IMPACT OF TRAUMA, 5-HOUR CONTINUING EDUCATION, SPONSORED BY GUARDIAN ANGEL, ILLINOIS HEALTH CARES, & UNIVERSITY OF ST FRANCIS (2012).

- Affiliations – PHI THETA KAPPA HONOR SOCIETY, MEMBER (2010-PRESENT); ALPHA DELTA NURSING HONOR

SOCIETY, MEMBER (2011-PRESENT); GUARDIAN ANGEL (2012).

ACHIEVEMENTS

- Successfully Completed Clinical Rotations in medical/surgical, telemetry, obstetrics, pediatrics, mental health, and ICU.

- Successfully Completed Preceptorship in the Emergency Room.

- Collaborated to Develop a Nursing Student Mentoring program: to provide support and resources for new nursing students. This program was developed in collaboration with Alpha Delta Nursing and the Nursing Student Association. I performed project management duties.

- Awarded the Harry and Henrietta Trackman Scholarship: for one semester in nursing school based on outstanding academic performance.

NURSING EXPERIENCE

Student Nurse, Clinical Rotations, DEF MEDICAL CENTER (Palatine, IL), ABC HOSPITAL (Chicago, IL) AND RST HOSPITAL (Rockford, IL). 10/2010 - 5/2012

- Four semesters of clinical rotations in various departments including, medical/surgical, telemetry, obstetrics, pediatrics, mental health, and ICU.

- Provided complete patient care for 1-2 patients per clinical day including, physical assessments, medication administration, wound care, and teaching.

Student Nurse, Preceptorship, XYZ Emergency Care Center, Highland Park, IL. 4/2012.

- Successfully completed preceptorship (40 hours) at ER

- Performed patient care from admission to discharge including physical assessments, medication administration, wound care, and teaching.

Data Entry Associate, ABC Insurance, Chicago, IL. July 2001—Feb 2005.

- Enter new customer application data and make changes to current applications.

OTHER NURSING SKILLS

- Care for patients including, observing and recording symptoms.

- Based on treatment plans, assess the progress of patients.
- Administer medications and injections. Routes include: PO, IV, INH, IM, Sub-q.
- Dress wounds and incisions.
- Perform routine laboratory work.
- Write and develop nursing care treatment plans.
- Teach patients about self-care to improve their health habits and quality of life.
- Assist patients and their families with compassionate support.
- Assure quality of care by adhering to therapeutic standards.
- Protect patients and employees by adhering to infection-control policies and protocols.
- Document patient care services by charting in-patient and department records.
- Maintain a safe and clean working environment by complying with hospital rules and procedures.
- Maintain communication among nursing teams by documenting and advising on actions taken.
- Nurture patient confidence with adherence to confidentiality.

Defense Contractor Résumé Sample

PROFILE

Detail-oriented and accomplished international logistics manager with six years of experience in cargo movements, large-scale transient operations, and passenger services. Knowledge of freight and cargo industry, as well as routing and transportation procedures. Track record of program leadership in challenging environments and high-pressure situations. Catalyst for organizational improvement through personnel management, motivation, and inspiration. Exceptional customer service and communication skills. An efficient manager, dedicated to fostering a working environment that encourages collaboration and optimizes team performance. Active Top Secret clearance.

COMPETENCIES

- Strategic Planning
- Project Management
- Procurement
- Information Management
- Staff Development
- Cargo Movements
- HAZMAT
- Radio Frequency Identification
- Quality Assurance

EDUCATION

- Bachelor of Arts in Management, ABC University, 2015

CERTIFICATIONS

- IBM Maximo Asset Management v7.5
- Procurement Supply Management Academy, Houston, TX

TECHNICAL

- Databases: Access, SCOPE, USH, Crystal and Spillman
- Office: MS Office Suite, MS Word, Excel, Power Point, Outlook,
- Government: Automated Message Handling Systems (AMHS), Defense Message Handling (DMH), Blue Force Tracking, Inter-

Theater Airlift Request System (ITARS), Single Mobility System (TRANSCOM)

- Logistics: Global Decision Support System (GDSS), Global Air Transportation Execution System (GATES), Product Management Transportation Information System (PM TIS), Integrated Booking System Container Management Module (IBS-CMM), RFID tagging, Transportation Control and Movement Documents (TCMD).

WORK EXPERIENCE

Sr. Movement/Cargo/Passenger Service Manager, DEF COMPANY, Herndon, VA, 2/2011-Present

Company Profile: Defense industry contractor with annual revenues of approximately $400M.

- Summary: While deployed on an overseas assignment in Afghanistan, I managed a team of 53 associates including company employees, foreign national subcontractors and assigned U.S. armed forces members that supported U.S Armed Forces operations.

- Managed cargo movement, passenger travel, in compliance with regulations and company procedures across air bases in Kuwait, Germany, Manas-Kyrgyzstan, Qatar, UAE, and Afghanistan to the U.S.

- Oversaw immigration and customs movement.

- Tracked flight status, organized travel and transportation, and managed material resources.

- Maintained reports, records, timecards, and equipment.

Accomplishments / Value Added

- Obtained a 25% reduction in workforce by driving re-staffing efforts to successfully deliver project goals.

- Received Certificate of Merit and Appreciation for exceptional performance and leadership.

Movement Control & Cargo/Passenger Service Specialist, IGHI COMPANY, Boston, MA, 1/2010-1/2011

Company Profile: Defense industry contractor with annual revenues of approximately $1B.

- Summary: While deployed on an overseas assignment in Afghanistan, I processed personnel travel and cargo movements, as well as provided access to classified information when requested by authorized personnel in my collateral role at Information Manager in support of U.S Armed Forces operations.

- Using the Global Decision Support System and Global Air Transportation Execution System software, I evaluated 45 short tons of cargo weekly to determine appropriate transportation mode, tracking status of flights and missions with the assistance of the U.S. Air Force.
- Coordinated processing of shipments and handling of Air Cargo Manifests.

Accomplishments / Value Added

- Ensured maximum customer satisfaction by providing quality service to Bagram Airfield and other customers.

Logistics Coordinator, MMG COMPANY, Laredo, TX, 1/2009-2/2010

Company Profile: Engineering, procurement, construction and services company with annual revenues of approximately $2B.

- Summary: While deployed on an overseas assignment in Afghanistan, I provided logistics coordination and document control services in support of U.S Armed Forces operations.
- Responsible for timely, efficient movement of cargo.
- Utilized proprietary and commercial logistics and supply management software to review invoices and shipping manifests for compliance with local customs and international regulations.
- Verified bench stock levels, confirmed lifecycles and warranties, and used United States General Services Administration (GSA) and Fed Log Army programs for ordering materials.
- Used Global Decision Support System and Global Air Transportation Execution System to track flight/mission statuses.
- Oversaw routing, recording, and oversight for office checks of engineering and supplier data.
- Liaised with reproduction department to expedite services as needed.
- Acquired key certified supplier data and technical documents, and managed daily requisition and P.O. entry.

Accomplishments / Value Added

- Ensured expedited cargo movement through efficient cargo processing and creating tracking control numbers.

- Innovated and implemented a project document control record keeping system.
- Revamped purchase order files to ensure current federal acquisition regulations (FAR) compliance for critical audits.

Area Supervisor, XYZ COMPANY, Norfolk, VA, 6/2004-11/2008

Company Profile: Defense industry contractor with annual revenues of approximately $2B.

- Summary: While deployed on overseas assignments in Kosovo, Romania & Bulgaria, I directed 288 linguists for unit briefings, and provided necessary materials for tasks in support of U.S Armed Forces operations.
- Orchestrated training, scheduling, logistics, and housing with strong focus on maintaining personnel health and welfare.
- Mentored staff throughout mission and project decommissioning.
- Developed situational reports and performance evaluations.
- Managed financial affairs with local banks and vendors.
- Accomplishments / Value Added
- Established field offices in Romania and Bulgaria.
- Spearheaded specialized military linguistics project in support of U.S Armed Forces operations.
- Championed recruitment program including creation of standard operating procedures for interviews and hiring.
- Ensured client satisfaction by serving as sole point-of-contact and maintaining focus on satisfaction of requirements.

Support Center Clerk, FRY COMPANY, Houston, TX, 5/2003-6/2004

Company Profile: Engineering, procurement, construction, and services company with annual revenues of approximately $3B.

- Summary: While deployed on an overseas assignment in Kosovo, I provided information and administrative support services in support of U.S. Peacekeeping and military operations.
- Distributed interdepartmental communications (e.g. memorandums, bulletin notifications, etc.) to the appropriate personnel.
- Managed the secure and non-secure communications within proprietary messaging systems.
- Oversaw the distribution of US and NATO Base ID badges.

- Handled delivery, return, and database management for civilian and military personnel.

- Accomplishments / Value Added

- Spearheaded Records Preservation Program including providing requested information services, supporting surge rotations and transfers of authority (TOA), and ensuring optimal inventory management.

LANGUAGE PROFICIENCIES

- English (Native and Fluent); Chinese, Cantonese (Native and Fluent); and French (Proficient).

Banking Résumé Sample

PROFILE

Award-winning, detail-oriented, and discreet Business Banker with six years of experience in relationship management, sales, and business development. Demonstrated record of acquiring and developing new, affluent, high-value clients. Dedicated, global view, hard-working, productive, meticulous, accurate, accountable, motivated to optimize, cost-conscious, effective under pressure, delegates effectively, mentor. Competence in both oral and written English to communicate in a clear and concise manner. Able to converse in Spanish and fluent in French.

COMPETENCIES

- Commercial Banking
- Credit / Non-Credit Products
- Corporate / Business Banking
- Trust / Treasury Management
- Financial Sales
- Portfolio Management
- Wealth Management
- Financial Advising
- Branch Management

EDUCATION

- B.S., Management, University of Denver, Denver, CO; 2007.
- Relevant Coursework: comprehensive studies in money and banking, fundamentals of finance, accounting, investments, marketing, and management and organizational behavior.

TECHNICAL

- Microsoft Office Suite, Word, Excel, PowerPoint, Outlook

EXPERIENCE

Relationship Banker, XYZ Bank, Long Lake, CA; 2012 - Present.

- Responsible for retaining and expanding client relationships and soliciting new business from existing and prospective clients designed to grow the bank's deposit and loan portfolios.

- Leverage referrals and other lead generation techniques (e.g., community outreach) to identify new prospects and cross-selling opportunities.

- Cultivate partnerships with specialist areas such as Financial Advisors, Small Business and Private Banking to obtain and provide qualified referrals.

- Ensured strict compliance with all internal and external State and Federal compliance rules, regulations, policies, procedures, guidelines, and laws.

Accomplishments / Value Add

- Generated new business with physicians, retail establishments, scientists, entrepreneurs, and lawyers by sourcing payroll, lines of credit, merchant services, commercial accounts and trust accounts.

- Generated new accounts work $200K of new deposits through cold-calling, outbound calls, and business client visits.

- Winner of Million Dollar Club and Sales & Service Excellence Awards: for generating new business for the bank.

Banking Business Specialist, New Bank, Whittier, CA; 2007 - 2012.

- Established positive long-term relationships with business owners, senior managers, and key corporate executives; conducted comprehensive business banking needs assessments; and identified commercial banking products that achieved the client's commercial banking goals

- Cultivated sourced multiple payroll and merchant opportunities, maintain a high level of customer service, and establish a pipeline of customer referrals to develop new client business.

Accomplishments / Value Add

- Sourced and closed on new business deals of $1.1 million, $1.5 million and a variety of other deals cumulatively totaling $6 million in commercial lending.

- Generated over $1.2 million in new investments by sourcing and developing a business relationship with a La Jolla-based, high-value client who previously had done business outside of banks.

- Winner of Million Dollar Club Award for consistently generating new business for the bank.

- Winner of Sales & Service Excellence Award for providing sales and support for all banking office business clients.

Personal Banker, MRW Bank, Eureka, CA; 2007 - 2009.

- Sold retail banking products and services to existing customers and new prospects.

- Provided broad base of financial and credit services with the goals of acquiring 100% of the customers' business.

Customer Sales and Service Representative, MRO Bank, Ojai CA; 2007.

- Responded to routine inquiries and complaints from internal and external customers regarding financial products, loans, credit lines and services.

- Researched and resolved routine to moderately complex problems and inquiries.

Sales Résumé Sample

PROFILE

Award-winning, educational sales executive with extensive experience in technology sales, territory development, business management and training with a compelling record of driving profitability.

CAREER SUMMARY

- Profile: Senior educational technology sales executive with over twenty years of experience in identifying technology products that offer high profit potential, prospecting for new clients, expanding territory, and building win-win partnerships. Possess an unprecedented sales record with significant educational clients. Three-time President's Circle winner for sales achievement.

- Sales Team Leadership: Leader and mentor of highly effective sales teams. Possesses the ability to develop talent, create demand for emerging educational products, and envision marketing campaigns that generate revenue pipelines and build market share.

- Organizational Style: A personable, enthusiastic, and mature manager who builds bridges and discovers moments of excellence to leverage opportunities for coaching a sales team in how to reach their potential.

KEY ACHIEVEMENTS

- **Generated over $3 Million in Sales over Five Years**: Created a go-to-market strategy for a new educational touch screen product, which resulted in over $3 million in sales over a five-year period.

- **Increased Sales Revenues from $400K to $1.1 Million annually**: Collaborated with sales, professional development staff and marketing to create a sales and marketing campaign to win business from the DEF Initiative, which resulted in sales revenues increasing in this area from $400K to $1.1 million annually.

- **Mentored a Sales Person Who Sold over $2 Million**: Mentored a sales person with no educational sales experience, teaching him how to sell educational technology into schools. He became a very successful sales rep, selling over $2 million in sales annually.

PROFESSIONAL EXPERIENCE

ABC Company, Omaha, NE, 4/2008-7/2015

Regional Sales Manager / Product Manager (10/2009-7/2015)

- Led business development, regional sales and product management for an Interactive Learning System for special education use and educational technology products such as SMART Boards, projectors and digital signage.

- Directly managed the U.S. reseller distribution network and direct sales in states where ABC didn't have reseller representation for a high-tech computer access product.

- Identified emerging educational hardware and software. Determined how to market these products to customers using a consultative selling approach.

- Created prospective customer databases to perform direct marketing and to assist resellers in their sales efforts.

- Collaborated with sales, professional development staff and marketing to create a sales and marketing campaign to win business from the Western Technology Initiative, which resulted in sales revenues increasing in this area from $400K to $1.1 million annually.

- Partnered with software publishers and created hardware and software product line extensions to continually improve the product and to add more features and capabilities.

Regional Sales Director – Educational Sales (4/2008-10/2009)

- Managed and trained the sales team to more effectively sell into K-12 education.

- Teamed with ABC's educational training manager to create a wider range of professional development programs for school customers.

- Mentored a marketing manager who had no previous experience in marketing to educational customers and trained her in using techniques that more effectively promoted products and services to educational customers.

- Mentored a sales person with no educational sales experience to sell into schools, teaching how to sell educational technology. Through my mentoring efforts, he became a very successful K-12 sales rep, selling over $2 million in sales and annually.

DEF Company, San Francisco, CA, 4/2003-4/2008

Entrepreneur / Sales Manager

- Sold and installed AV equipment that supported the electronic presentation of faculty content (Powerpoint, websites, etc.) for university classrooms; SMART interactive whiteboards in K-12 classrooms; and digital messaging systems for school and community public access television stations.

- Managed all aspects of a 10-person company, including project management of customer installation projects, sales, back office functions, ordering, inventory control and cash flow.

- The company earned exclusive installer status at FGU University, installing or updating the electronic presentation equipment in over 150 classrooms on campus.

XYZ Company, Green Bay, WI, 11/1981-4/2003

Educational Sales Representative

- Lead and mentored a field sales team that sold Apple computers, computer furniture, presentation monitors, LCD panels/projectors, interactive video, and installed presentation classrooms in Wisconsin K-12 schools and universities.

- Earned the President's Circle Award for 110+% sales quota achievement three times.

TECHNICAL SKILLS

- Design: Camtasia Studio, Matchware Mediator, Microsoft Movie Maker, Paint Shop Pro, Audacity audio editor, SMART Notebook, Dragon Naturally Speaking, Ewisoft Website Builder, SMART Table Toolkit development software, Publisher, Tightrope Media Carousel, Display Changer, Amplify Playlist Builder.

- Marketing: MyEmma, Mail Chimp, Survey Monkey, Market Data Retrieval, InfoUSA, US Department of Education databases, EBSCO databases, Filemaker Pro, ACT, Connectwise (CRM).

- Productivity: Microsoft Word, Excel, Powerpoint, Calendar and Outlook, Nuance PDF Converter Pro, Nuance Create! Assistant, Google Drive, Lenovo SHAREit.

EDUCATION

- M.B.A.- Marketing – Keller Graduate School of Management (Chicago, IL)

Web Designer Résumé Sample

PROFILE

Widely experienced Windows and web developer / designer and project leader. Offer extensive experience developing, implementing and supporting business applications and dynamic gaming contests. Expert level of proficiency with ASP.NET, C#, PHP, Windows Forms, JavaScript, CSS, jQuery, MySQL and MSSQL to architect systems that increase efficiency, enhance performance and allow clients to achieve critical objectives.

CORE COMPETENCIES

- Project Leadership
- Website Design / SEO
- Process Automation
- Production Web Servers
- Application Development
- Image / Video Editing

SUMMARY

- **Solutions focused** – view time-consuming processes and system shortfalls as opportunities to innovate. Developed numerous systems at Facebook, Intel, Microsoft and Prudential Securities that automated processes, increased quality of information and provided instant access to business critical data.

- **Technically savvy** – continuously adapt to evolving requirements and drive adoption of emerging technology. Increased efficiency of profitability tracking by building and maintaining a Management Dashboard web application – a system that has been widely regarded as one of the company's most valuable tools.

- **Skilled communicator** – explain often-complex concepts / processes in a clear, benefits-focused manner. Created user manuals and technical documentation for almost every application developed, which reduced transition times and ensured outstanding end-user experiences.

EXPERIENCE

Senior Developer – ABC Company, Newark, NJ, 05/2013 – Present

- Developed multiple types of websites.

- Integrated sites with FaceBook's SDK that enables users to login via FaceBook, and add "Like" buttons as well as other Social Media plugins.

- Enhanced sites with internal APIs (e.g., cURL calls) to permit the checking of geolocation based on IP, and allow users to login, check user balances & check age requirement for the contests.

- Created translation files so the sites could be displayed in different languages.

- Technical Environment: PHP, MySQL, JavaScript, CSS, cURL, jQuery plugins, XML

Senior Developer – XYZ Agency, Scottsdale, AZ, 08/2005 – 05/2013

- Developed and managed systems to support the finance team / CFO. Managed all requests for the Management Dashboard system, Billings & Revenue and Performics. Built prototypes for new projects and user guides / manuals for completed projects.

- Built and maintained a Management Dashboard System. Enhanced the popular reporting system by creating a module that saved the finance team several hours a day.

- Coded middle-tier, Class Libraries to incorporate business logic and provide data access to several data sources.

- Developed and oversaw SQL Server Stored Procedures, Triggers, Views, DTS and SSIS Packages.

- Reduced development times by architecting a standard login for all applications using web services.

- Technical Environment: ASP.NET, C#, JavaScript, CSS, jQuery, SQL, Windows Forms, XML

Senior Programmer Analyst – Washington DC, 07/2003 – 08/2005

- Developed order tracking and inventory management applications. Developed SQL tables, views, roles and stored procedures for all .NET projects. Partnered in deploying the company's ecommerce site.

- Designed the Cost System, which provided production managers the ability to calculate freight, customs and royalty charges for inventory purchases.

- Created and maintained an Request Online system, which provided the Creative Department the ability to easily track and manage art requests.
- Technical Environment: ASP.NET, ADO.NET, C#, JavaScript, SQL, XML, MS Access, Crystal Reports

Project Leader – RS Corporation – Minneapolis, MN, 06/1997 – 11/2002

- Led and developed a five-member development team to successfully deliver and manage several large-scale projects, including a career development tracking system, business plan websites, a time reporting system and several attendance reporting websites.
- Designed, coded and managed RS's Financial Career Development Program – a two year project that produced a 50-screen website, enabling the ability to track Financial Advisor development.
- Designed and coded RS's Domestic and International Financial Advisor Business Plan websites, which used CICS transactions to retrieve and save information entered by Financial Advisors.
- Built a Computer Based Training (CBT) tracking application that determined which Financial Advisors (FA) were eligible for CBTs, tracked the FA's progress and charged branches the appropriate fees upon completion.
- Technical Environment: DHTML, JavaScript, XML, XSLT, VBScript, ActiveX, CICS, COBOL, HTML, ASP

EDUCATION

- BA, Information Systems, Columbia University New York, 1997.

TECHNICAL EXPERTISE

- Programming Languages: C#, JavaScript, Transact-SQL, ASP.NET, jQuery, Ajax, CSS, Visual Basic, HTML, DHMTL, ASP, VBScript, ADO, ADO.NET, XML, XSLT, JAVA, CICS, COBOL, C++, PHP, MySQL, Silverlight
- Software: Microsoft Visual Studio 2010, SQL Server 2008, Crystal Reports, Telerik .NET Controls, Janus .NET Controls, Infragistics .NET Controls, Microsoft Office Suite (Word, Excel), Microsoft SourceSafe
- Design Tools: Adobe CS5 (Photoshop, Premiere, After Effects, Flash)

Technical Résumé Sample

PROFILE

Dedicated and skilled Software Test Engineer and Quality Assurance Specialist with extensive experience in the complete software development lifecycle, complex analysis activities, software testing, test case creation and execution, cross-functional collaboration. A passion for contributing advanced knowledge in all facets of testing. Dynamic communicator skilled at cultivating solid professional relationships and using diverse technologies to power the testing experience.

AREAS OF EXPERTISE

- Software Testing
- Testing Infrastructure
- Design & Implementation
- Quality Assurance
- SET Black Box Testing
- Manual Testing
- Delivery Process Improvements
- Defect & Bug Tracking

TECHNICAL STRENGTHS

- Platforms: Microsoft Windows 8, 7, 2003/2008, XP
- Web Frameworks: JavaScript, JQuery, SOAP, REST
- Databases: TSQL, SQL Server, MySQL
- Languages: Java SE, HTML, CSS, Perl, Visual C#, Object Oriented Programming, Selenium WebDriver
- Productivity Tools: Visual Studio, Eclipse, Microsoft Office, Microsoft Project
- Testing Framework: JMeter, Selenium WebDriver, Nunit, Junit, TestNG, ANT, White Testing Framework

EDUCATION AND CERTIFICATIONS

- Bachelor of Science in Technology, Illinois University, Chicago IL
- Online Coursework: Selenium Webdriver, JMeter, JavaScript, JQuery

- C# Programming 1 & 2, C# Automation 1, Bellevue College Continuing Education
- MCP Certified Professional, MS Certification
- CompTIA Network + Certified
- CompTIA A+ Certified

EXPERIENCE

ABC Company, Brookington, IA, Jan. 2014 to Sept. 2014

Software Test Engineer

- Sole test engineer for a start-up software development company with responsibility for performing manual and automated testing against a Microsoft Office Application.
- Authored and managed MSTest automated test cases.
- Meticulously created test cases and bug reports using Visual Studio Online.
- Presented the benefits of Visual Studio Online as a robust test case and bug tracking management tool.
- Maximized the use of VMware to test daily builds and release builds against diverse systems.
- Utilized C# to create automated unit test case suites against existing code.

DEF Corporation, Redmond, WA, Apr. 2005 to Dec. 2013

Software Test Engineer III, 2013

- Contracted to run manual test scripts against the XBoxOne console in addition to directly supporting a Software Development Engineer in Test (SDET) to ensure on-time XBoxOne delivery.
- Meticulously created and regressed bugs, and produced daily automated reports.
- Recognized for expeditiously ramping up console workings and the tools utilized for testing.
- Rapidly learned and applied existing automation to execute test scripts.
- Collaborated with SDETs and members of the testing team to correct, run, and verify test scripts.

Software Test Engineer II, 2012-2013

- Contracted to spearhead the test automation process, and to ensure no testing issues.

- Closely tracked automation testing operations and immediately resolved any errors.

- Eliminated bug defects not handled directly by the automated test process.

- Directed parts of the testing of unique system builds, which led to the expedited testing of software and enhanced team productivity.

Software Test Engineer I, 2005-2012

- Selected to test connectivity and accuracy between the Xbox console and website, which required developing a manual test plan for three web-based applications.

- Worked in partnership with Project Managers to execute tests of the web based application.

- Introduced a manual test script that included more than 100 test cases for 14 distinct web pages.

- Implemented manual test scripts that identified basic UI errors to in-depth logic errors in code.

- Ameliorated pre-existing test scripts directly resulting in the realization and correction of previously undiscovered issues and software bugs. Product reliability was subsequently extended.

GHI Agency, Seattle, WA, Dec. 2002 to May 2005

Software Test Engineer

- Successfully led the design, development, and implementation of test plans, which led to quality of software components and processes throughout data center migration from Seattle, WA to Reston, VA.

- Developed test plans and cases customized for desktop and web-based application testing related to a medical surveillance system.

- Documented before and after migration data, ran identical tests, and authenticated identical results.

- Maximized the use of Java and Selenium Webdriver to create automation test scripts, and worked in partnership with Software Developers to verify and fix issues.

- Proposed testing tools that were adopted by the agency and contributed to the project's success.

- Devised Selenium Webdriver scripts to run tests on webpages in Internet Explore and Firefox.

JKL Corporation, Bellevue, WA, Dec. 2005 to Jun. 2011

Software Test Engineer/Quality Assurance Engineer

- Diligently tested desktop and client server applications for the Cardio Schedule, Apollo LX, registries, and reporting projects.
- Led the comprehensive testing life cycle of the Cardio Schedule and Reports Project in alignment with project objectives and ahead of schedule.

Manufacturing Résumé Sample

OVERVIEW

Highly effective, growth-oriented, business executive who blends operational experience and decisive leadership to drive improved productivity while reducing costs, lead-time, and inventory to deliver high quality products on-time. P&L responsibility up to $60 million. Extensive experience in directing manufacturing operations, strategic planning, financial analysis, plant consolidations, and successful product launches. Possess exceptional planning, organizational, and delegation skills and uniquely qualified to be a creative leader in business affairs. A personable staff manager who is dedicated to communicating the urgency of corporate mission, core values and vision. A champion of fostering an environment that encourages collaboration to optimize team performance.

KEY OPERATIONAL OUTCOMES

- Improved productivity by 17% via implementation of a performance-based incentive plan.

- Reduced Lead Times by 30% and on time delivery by 25% through Lean activities.

- Drove inventory reductions of 27% by supporting Configure to Order (CTO) implementation of various products through SKU reduction, education, and interaction with sales and suppliers.

- Achieved significant waste reduction through execution of Kaizen events from Value Stream Mapping.

PROFESSIONAL EXPERIENCE

ABC Company, Boise, ID, 5/2015-3/2016

VP of Operations

- Managed an 80,000 sq. ft. furniture manufacturing facility with 160+ employees. Directed the operations function, including production, engineering, materials management, safety, scheduling and facilities. Annual budget of $23M.

- Drove productivity improvement initiatives that yielded a 30% lead time reduction and a 25% ontime delivery improvement through the implementation of Lean initiatives.

- Completed major shop floor moves on time, within budget, and with zero negative impact to customers, resulting in increased capacity and fewer manpower hours required.

DEF Company, Chicago, IL, 5/2005-5/2015

Director of Operations, (2009-2015)

- Directed all aspects of manufacturing operations at a 475,000 sq. ft. facility with 300+ employees. Leadership included production, materials management, process engineering, quality, safety, and environmental sustainability. Annual budget of $60M.
- Collaborated with sister manufacturing plant to implement regional manufacturing, resulting in a $1M+ cost reduction in the first year.
- Delivered $500K+ annually in productivity and materials cost reductions in fiscal years 2011, 2012 and 2013 as a result of the implementation of standardized work, process improvements and improved velocity.
- Quality PPM reduced by 75% since 2009.

Senior Director, Product Management, (2008-2009)

- Introduced and launched 3 new successful product offerings on time and under budget, contributing $2.3M to bottom line profitability.
- Maximized productivity by improving work efficiencies, resulting in reducing time-to-market from 24 months to 18 months for complex product offerings.

Director, Operations and Engineering, (2007-2008)

- P&L responsibility for two manufacturing facilities with 600+ employees. Combined annual budget of $48M.
- Achieved significant waste reduction through execution of Kaizen events from Value Stream Mapping.
- Improved productivity by 17% via the implementation of a performance-based incentive plan.
- Reduced inventory by 11% through implementation of complexity reduction and common parts strategy.

Director, Planning and Controls, DEF Company (2005-2007)

- Oversight of seven manufacturing facilities, managing multiple teams of program managers, material managers, production schedulers, and process engineers.

- Implemented common processes across functional areas when manufacturing facilities were transitioned from individual profit centers to combined shared services.

- Developed policies, procedures, and material control systems to reduce costs, streamline procedures, and implement solutions.

- Directed the closure of manufacturing facility including the transfer of work to US-based facilities.

Business Development Manager, (2005)

- Developed customers throughout the sales cycle, from proposal to price negotiations and closing the deal.

- Added 2 major customers prior to position being eliminated after 6 months due to business unit integration.

XYZ Corporation, West Palm Beach, FL, 1/1997-5/2005

Director, Business Operations Support / Global Planning Group (2002-2005)

- Responsible for monthly Sales, Inventory and Operations Planning (SIOP) and analysis of revenue outlook, identifying and resolving issues relating to critical components required to meet $870M annual revenue plan.

- Managed Global Planning group responsible for monthly production schedules for 15+ top-line products based on regional demand plans, supplier capacity and inventory position.

- Worked closely with EMS providers with respect to manufacturing and delivery issues, reducing standard lead times from 14 to 10 days while maintaining 98%+ on time delivery.

Senior Product Line Manager (1999-2002)

- Responsible for managing all aspects of planning, development, and lifecycle management of highest volume and/or revenue retail POS terminals and peripherals that drove $160M in annual revenue.

- Managed cross-functional, Product Release Team consisting of HW and SW engineering, marketing, customer services, operations, quality, manufacturing, and other support organizations.

Senior Pricing Analyst (1997-1999)

- Financial analysis of retail customer bid proposals through major bid review process.

- Identified and assessed financial impact and risks of non-standard terms and conditions.
- Supported Product Management in new product development and introduction, including pricing strategy, competitive analysis, capital budgeting decisions, and product positioning.

TECHNICAL SKILLS

- MS Office Suite
- MRP systems
- Financial Analysis, CapEx

EDUCATION

- MBA, Finance – University of California, Santa Barbara, CA
- B.S., Business Administration – University of Minnesota, Minneapolis, MN

About the Author

Randall Scasny is the Director of HowToGetHiredQuickly.com, a job search assistance service that services job seekers experiencing difficult career transitions.

Previously, Mr. Scasny held a variety of technical and managerial positions in Fortune 500 companies. Mr. Scasny is a U.S. Navy veteran, having served on the USS Manitowoc, USS Inflict, and USS Yosemite in various locations around the world.

He holds degrees from Western Illinois University and The New Mexico Institute of Mining and Technology. Mr. Scasny grew up in Hartford, WI, a graduate of Hartford Union High School.

Mr. Scasny can be contacted through his website:

http://www.HowToGetHiredQuickly.com

You can email him at mail@howtogethiredquickly.com

www.ingramcontent.com/pod-product-compliance
Lightning Source LLC
Chambersburg PA
CBHW022115170526
45157CB00004B/1649